10/20

MORE
THAN
READY

MORE THAN READY

Be Strong and Be You, and Other Lessons for Women of Color on the Rise

CECILIA MUÑOZ

SEAL PRESS
New York

Seal Press
Hachette Book Group
1290 Avenue of the Americas, New York, NY 10104
sealpress.com @sealpress

Printed in the United States of America

First Edition: April 2020

Published by Seal Press, an imprint of Perseus Books, LLC, a subsidiary of Hachette Book Group, Inc. The Seal Press name and logo is a trademark of the Hachette Book Group.

Some names and identifying details have been changed to protect the privacy of individuals.

The Hachette Speakers Bureau provides a wide range of authors for speaking events. To find out more, go to www.hachettespeakersbureau.com or call (866) 376-6591.

The publisher is not responsible for websites (or their content) that are not owned by the publisher.

Print book interior design by Jeff Williams.

Library of Congress Cataloging-in-Publication Data
Names: Muñoz, Cecilia, author.
Title: More than ready : be strong and be you ... and other lessons for women of color on the rise / Cecilia Muñoz.
Description: First edition. | New York : Seal Press, 2020.
Identifiers: LCCN 2019048874 | ISBN 9781580059480 (hardcover) | ISBN 9781580059497 (ebook)

Subjects: LCSH: Minority women—Psychology. | Minority women in the professions. | Success.

Classification: LCC HQ1161 .M86 2020 | DDC 305.48/8—dc23

LC record available at https://lccn.loc.gov/2019048874

ISBNs: 978-1-58005-948-0 (hardcover); 978-1-58005-949-7 (ebook)

LSC-C

10 9 8 7 6 5 4 3 2 1

Gracias, Katty and Eduardo,
for making it all possible.

Thank you, Amit,
for bringing me joy every day.

Tina and Meera,
this is for you, with love.

CONTENTS

AUTHOR'S NOTE

I OWE A GREAT DEAL TO THE SEVEN WOMEN WHO GENER-ously shared their stories and insights with me as I was preparing this book. I conducted the interviews in person or by phone, and with their permission, I took detailed notes and used a taping service to record our conversations. This made it possible for me to include extensive excerpts and share the women's words with you as I heard them.

While writing this book, I gave a lot of thought to the choice of words that I used to describe the community that I am a part of. Some prefer to call ourselves "Hispanic," which refers to our ancestry in the Spanish-speaking world. Others prefer "Latino," which refers to our geographic origins in Latin America. Neither fully captures who we are, so for decades I have used both terms interchangeably, which is what I ultimately chose to do in this book.

This decision does not come without complications. Using "Latino" is problematic in particular because Spanish is a gendered language; for years, I have used "Latino" when I am referring to a man, "Latina," when I mean a woman, and "Latino/a" when it could be one or the other. For the purposes of this book, I have traded the awkward "Latino/a" for the recently invented "Latinx," which describes the community in a gender-neutral way.

I am aware that this is a controversial choice. People who use "Latinx" make the case that we should adapt our language to be as inclusive as we can, making room for men, women, and people who don't conform to traditional ideas of gender. They point out that language has the power both to reflect the ways in which the world is changing and to pave the way for that change. Others argue that "Latinx" is a word invented outside of our community in an unwelcome attempt to change a language that many of us have fought to preserve. They rightly point out that "Latinx" is a term that most of the community wouldn't recognize and may not accept.

I am respectful of and sympathetic to both arguments, and I wrestled with the decision. I believe in the power of language enough to have spent a lifetime insisting that we use it in a way that opens doors—and minds—to women. In the end, I concluded that the people in my family and community who don't conform to either gender deserve the same. I found using a new and unfamiliar word uncomfortable at first, and you might, too. We'll adjust. That's the point.

INTRODUCTION

SONIA SOTOMAYOR. ILEANA ROS-LEHTINEN. MAE CAROL Jemison. Carole Moseley Braun. Condoleezza Rice. Deb Haaland. Sharice Davids. Pramila Jayapal. Geisha Williams. Urusla Burns.

These women of color share something remarkable. They are all "firsts": the first Latina Supreme Court justice (Sotomayor) and congresswoman (Ros-Lehtinen); the first African American female astronaut (Jemison), senator (Moseley Braun), and secretary of state (Rice); the first Native American and South Asian American women elected to Congress (Haaland, Davids, Jayapal); and the first Latina (Williams) and Black (Burns) women to lead Fortune 500 companies. The other thing they all have in common is that they served or are serving in our lifetimes. We watch them as they make their way and write their own histories. Each of them is doing it without a script, with no guide to lead the way and little in the way of precedents.

I have witnessed many such firsts. I knew the late Congresswoman Patsy Mink, a Japanese American from Hawaii who was the first woman of color ever elected to the United States Congress, and I remember when the late Shirley Chisholm, the first

African American congresswoman, ran for president. I am one of few Latinas who have ever served as an assistant to the president of the United States, and the first to lead the White House Domestic Policy Council, where I served in the West Wing under President Obama. My predecessor, the wonderful Melody Barnes, was the first African American woman in the same role. As women of color, we are among a generation accomplishing firsts—whether the first in our families to attend college, enter a traditional workplace, or embark on a nontraditional path. We have forged new roads, often without role models of our own, because we had no other choice. There was nobody that looked like us or who grew up like us taking on these roles before we did. Our stories have largely not been written because they are still unfolding.

Just as we are often firsts, it's not unusual for us also to be "onlies": the only woman in the room; the only person of color; and the only one bringing our particular set of experiences and expertise to our workplaces, classrooms, and teams—the various circles in which we conduct our lives. Sometimes being a first or an only means that we doubt ourselves. We wonder whether we really belong in these spaces and whether what we bring to them is enough. The moment we open our mouths, we may feel that we are not only speaking for ourselves but may be understood to be speaking for everyone like us. That's a lot of weight to carry. It can feel like a lot of responsibility.

I know this because I hear it all the time. It happens whenever I'm speaking in public, recounting my experiences as a woman of color who has spent a life in public service. When I give a speech to a group of young professionals or students, or lead a training for people in mid-career, we have the public part of the conversation, and then quietly, when the speech is over, I hear from you. You're the young African American woman who comes up to me while people are clearing out, takes my hand, and says, "Thank you for raising what it's like to be the only woman of color in the room. I'm that person all the time, and you named what I feel." You're the Asian American woman who says, "I'm glad you reminded the crowd that we're not all foreigners. I'm from Ohio, and I'm tired of people thinking I'm not an American." You're the Latina law student who sends me an email asking, "Why can't we find a prominent Latina to come and speak to our group? Why are there so few to choose from?" You're the Native American teacher who pulls me aside and whispers, "You included us in what you said. Nobody ever does that."

Your questions and observations are what gave me the courage to begin to write this book. You made me believe that I might have something useful and maybe even inspirational to offer, that maybe by writing a book I could engage with a lot more women beginning their own journeys and creating their own paths through a world they will change just by virtue of their presence. The world won't make it easy—there will be obstacles— but sharing what I have learned might help reduce obstacles of our own making. Maybe you won't have to learn the same lessons I learned the hard way.

Whether you are just starting your journey from home or from college into the bigger world, a few years into a job you're not sure you want to make your career, or in a career and wondering what your next steps might be, this book is for you. If you occasionally hear a voice inside your head or out in the world that questions what you have to offer or sows seeds of doubt, this is your book. If you sometimes feel that you're the only one who has days when you wonder whether you're in the right place or equipped to do what's in front of you, you will find in these pages that you're not alone.

I offer you insights and advice from a career in which I have often been a first or an only in the room, and from my experience balancing that career with my life as wife, mother, sibling, daughter, and friend. There are insights and advice that stem from my successes, but especially from my mistakes, anxieties, and missteps; the things I'm proud to have accomplished; and the things I wished I'd known how to do differently. You will make your own mistakes, too, but perhaps these insights will help you discern the lessons they offer, shake them off, and forge your own path forward.

Along my path, I have had the extraordinary privilege of coming to know some amazing women of color who have inspired me along the way. I include the results of candid conversations with some of them here. They include lawyers, educators, a public health professional, activists, nonprofit executives, and a congresswoman. These women were generous with their stories, triumphs, heartbreak, and wisdom. Sometimes their experiences provided lessons like mine and sometimes they taught me a thing or two. I am grateful that I can now pass on their insights to you, along with my own.

In this book I try to be as honest as I can about what I have experienced and overcome as a Latina in arenas dominated by white men. I share stories about first starting out and what influenced my decisions at the various points when I changed direction. I describe the times I doubted that I was up to the job or feared having to say the difficult thing when I was the only Latina in the room and I knew others wouldn't understand. I offer my own account, and accounts from the other women of color I spoke with for this book, about how we managed to get through those times when we doubted ourselves and the tactics we use to face our fears. I describe what I've learned about toughness and kindness; surviving setbacks; and balancing work, family, and life in general.

Weaving together stories from my decades of work in the Latinx civil rights movement and the eight years I spent on the senior team of the Obama White House, this book draws lessons from some of the challenges, large and small, that are part of my story and yet not at all unique to me. I have been the short woman literally elbowing her way into a circle of tall, male colleagues; the target of criticism from within my own community; and the midwestern Latina patiently explaining my community to the senator who complimented my English. I have discovered that other women were watching out for me while I wasn't looking, and I have learned how to pay it forward. I have raised two biracial daughters who add their own voices to the story, highlighting both how far we have come and how much further we have to go.

I'm guessing that you might be like me. I wasn't always sure of myself. Many times, I hesitated to put myself forward, wondering whether I would get it right. I worried about making mistakes and compensated by trying to look the part, reaching for perfection, doing the work, and being ultra-prepared. I have heard that same whisper in my ear that you likely have heard, the voice that tries to convince me that my experience isn't particularly valuable, that maybe having my voice in the room doesn't really matter, and that maybe I don't really belong there.

This book is about helping you hear a different voice—your own, strong voice—and to remind you that what you bring into any room is valuable. We can and must be seen and heard. For too long, decisions that affect every aspect of our lives have been made by others who often don't understand us or what we know about the world. It's time to step up. The world needs what we bring.

We are more than ready.

No matter what your profession, vocation, or field of endeavor, if you are a woman looking to blaze your own trail and forge your own firsts, and if you are wondering whether your life and experiences matter or whether what you bring with you as you begin your journey is enough, you are not alone. May you find good company in this book, and the tools to help you make your way while celebrating—and never compromising—who you are.

Chapter 1

STARTING OUT

IF THERE IS SUCH A THING AS A "TYPICAL" LATINA, I AM NOT IT. Most of us live west of the Mississippi River; I was born in Michigan. Most US Hispanics have roots in the southwestern United States, Mexico, or the Caribbean; my family is from Bolivia, right smack in the middle of South America. People of Hispanic origin don't even come close to looking alike because we have roots in the Americas, Africa, and Europe, but we are understood in the US to be brown. I am a product of that history, but you wouldn't necessarily know that to look at me. Like many Latinx people, I have ancestors who were indigenous Americans, but I look more like my ancestors who came to Latin America from Europe, some of them centuries ago and some as recently as my maternal grandfather, who traveled to Bolivia from Spain in the early twentieth century. The ñ in my name is a marker of who I am. I have spent a lifetime explaining it, insisting on it, and teaching people how to type it. I have given up on teaching people how to pronounce Muñoz. (They seem to prefer MOON-yohz, but it's moon-YOHZ.)

You, too, are a product of your history, whether you know much about that history or not. It shapes who you are in overt ways that the rest of us can see and in subtler ways below the surface. I consider myself lucky that I know something about my family's roots. Not everyone can say the same. And some of the history of how each of us got here—to this exact moment in the precise place where you are sitting with this book—is glorious and some of it is painful.

Those of us with immigrant heritage often carry echoes of the choices that led our families to leave their homes and strike out for a new place. So many of us descend from people who didn't leave their homes to come to America by choice at all—they were taken by force. Still others descend from people for whom America was home, and they were removed from their lands by force. We all still live with the legacy of that brutal history, especially those who are its direct descendants. Pretty much by definition, because we are women of color, we are at most only a few generations removed from people who showed extraordinary resilience and strength and who endured what seems unendurable. Our ancestors were survivors and strivers, generation after generation. That's how we got here. We are their legacy.

Dr. Maya Angelou, the poet, novelist, and all-around wise woman, once told an interviewer from *Huffington Post Black Voices* that you have no way of knowing where you're going if you don't know where you've been. "The more you know of your history," she said, "the more liberated you are." I think it matters to have a sense of where you come from, even if you don't have a lot of specific information about your forebears. We know we are the products of certain forces of history, even if we can't name many of our ancestors. And, of course, all of us bring our own personal history to every room we're in. We may be the products of a set of historical trends, or descendants of some major diaspora, or not, but each of us is also someone from a family, neighborhood, and community. Our identity is the result of a lot of forces, but it is also uniquely our own. We bring all of it with us wherever we go.

I think of this identity as a major source of strength and a foundation from which to grow. In the moments when I am most challenged, I'm not sure if I'm succeeding, and I don't know what kind of person people are seeing when they look at me, I am conscious of my ability to reach back and know who I am in some kind of deep way. I can see the person my family and friends see when I walk into a room. Whatever your circumstances, you are the product of a great chain of people, history, and forces that led to this moment and to you. It's worth taking time to reflect on it and build it into your arsenal of things to draw on when you need sources of courage.

That is not to say that I always fully comprehended who I am. All of us go through a journey to understand ourselves and what we bring to the world, particularly when we're young adults. My own understanding of myself as a Latina has developed in stages, owing largely to the fact that I grew up in a place where there weren't many of us.

My parents came to Michigan as newlyweds in 1950. We were joined in the Detroit area by a collection of aunts, uncles, and cousins, which is how the United States became home to my family. Family was our major social circle; my school-age sleepovers were exclusively with my cousins—sleepovers with anyone else were kind of unthinkable—and they were made magical by my mother's exotic stories about growing up in the eastern part of Bolivia, which is in the Amazon basin. There were some terrific stories involving snakes and caimans, but my favorites were the tales of the way my grandmother and aunts seemed able to sense when their loved ones were in danger, even from miles away. The stories were spectacular, full of menacing jungles and lurking jaguars. But the moral of the story was always connection: we are connected to one another no matter where we are, because we are family.

My siblings and I grew up bilingual, but like most kids in immigrant families, the Spanish began to fade as we got older and used it less. I have a distinct memory of the day I arrived at kindergarten and discovered that none of the other kids spoke Spanish. It was a startling revelation to me. Wanting to fit in, I switched to English with lightning speed. We understood ourselves as Americans—Michiganders and Midwesterners. We also understood ourselves as Bolivians—we often described ourselves as Spanish because nobody had ever heard of Bolivia and because language was a main marker for who we were, along with the exotic foods that we occasionally brought in our lunches (it's quite possible that the only empanadas in all of Detroit in that era were produced in our kitchen).

Michigan didn't offer much in the way of a Hispanic community. This was the 1970s, and there weren't many of us in the Detroit area. I don't need to use both hands to count the number of Latinx students and faculty I got to know during my four years at the University of Michigan. So, when I got to graduate school at the University of California at Berkeley, the diversity blew my mind. There were immigrants from Mexico and Central America, along with Mexican Americans whose history in the country went back generations. Suddenly, this thing that had felt so exotic and unique in Michigan—the ñ, the language, and the culture—was everywhere, even in the names of the places and the streets. Suddenly there were things that I didn't have to explain about myself because people *knew*. It was exhilarating.

I don't want to overstate it; Hispanic American culture is a very diverse and complicated thing. Bolivia is far from the places where most Latinx people have roots—the Caribbean, Mexico, Central America, or the Southwestern US—and there is a great deal that is different about the cultures, some of it trivial (a *torta* is a sandwich for a Mexican and a cake for me, as I learned to my chagrin the first time I ordered one) and some of it profound. Nevertheless, what I found during those years was a sense of community with other people who were products of the same historical phenomena: the impact of the Spanish colonizers of the Americas and the consequences of their interactions with both the indigenous people they encountered there and the people they kidnapped from Africa and enslaved there.

The diversity of people who spring from that experience is breathtaking. And for a variety of reasons, a lot of us have roots in the United States—in some cases, roots that go back 500 years. Hispanic America may not be a monolithic thing, but we are a thing. I discovered the vastness and beauty of the US Latinx community, that I belonged to it and it belonged to me, when I lived in California. And the excitement I felt in discovering where I belonged also began to reveal to me the kind of work I wanted to do in my life beyond Berkeley.

Find What Is Yours to Do

I am fortunate in that my life and work often put me in the path of young people of color, particularly women, in forums that give them a chance to tell me what's on their minds and ask for guidance. The questions I get the most often fall into two categories.

The first is about what kinds of credentials and experience I think are the right ones to forge a particular career path, especially for people who are interested in some kind of public service and some way of making a difference. People want to know what I think should go on their resumes.

The second kind of question is broader. I get asked whether I believe change is possible and whether I think the people I am sitting with can be a part of that change, given the distressing state of the world right now.

For me, the same answer applies to both kinds of questions. Whether you do it through your job or through some other aspect of your life, you already possess the power to make a difference in the world. And the world needs you! It is full of challenges to be met and problems in need of the right people to apply themselves to find solutions. There are as many ways to go about making a difference as there are people. Your job is to figure out what is yours to do.

To me, this job is more important than the credentials on your resume or the grades you got in school. I would never talk someone out of going to college, though I will say that some of the smartest people I have ever known did not have college degrees, starting with my mother. I have talked more than one person out of going to law school, though I think a career in law is an excellent way to make a difference. These people were asking whether that credential on their resume might propel them into the right job. The trouble was that they didn't want to be lawyers. There is no single formula for success, and there are infinite pathways to having an impact on the world, whether you do it as a career or as a passion outside of your work life. The key is knowing yourself and what energizes you enough to make you want to engage.

Think of a straight horizontal line made up of an infinite number of points, and each of those points is a way to make a difference. There are career-focused ways to make a difference, like teaching at a school, joining a firm that is pioneering clean energy, working in a hospital, or leading your company's effort to develop effective diversity and inclusion efforts. I think of those as being at one end of the horizontal line. On the other end are other ways of making a difference that aren't how you make your living: joining your block association, participating in a group that is trying to change a law by writing to your legislature, taking a turn when your congregation organizes meals for people in need, or showing up at a march or rally. All of it matters. We need good people at every point on the continuum. The question for you is, which point feels like the work that you're meant to do?

As someone who has hired a lot of people in the past thirty years, when I see people who really love the work they are engaging in or hope to take on, it shows. It practically shines right through them. In that situation I'm much less concerned with what's on their resumes except insofar as their experiences give them a chance to tell me the story of why they love this work. The inverse is also true: it's not hard to spot someone who is looking for a credential on his or her resume but doesn't have that spark of enthusiasm for the work.

I don't mean to suggest that this determination is easy. It isn't. Sometimes it takes a little experimentation to find what feels like yours to do in the world. Sometimes following your heart means taking an unconventional path and doing something that nobody else is doing. Especially if you feel like you're swimming against the tide, it can help to know you're trying to be true to your spot on that continuum and doing what is yours to do.

Learn by Doing

I not only built a connection to my own community during the years that I lived in California but also stumbled upon what would become my career path, though I don't think I knew it at the time. This may sound like unconventional career advice, but I highly recommend being open to discovering what you are meant to do by accident. This strategy has worked for an astonishing number of people I know, including me.

My pathway into my life's work started through service. I was fortunate enough to get a scholarship to support two years of graduate school, which meant that I didn't have to wash dishes or shelve library books to support myself anymore. I could invest that time doing community-focused volunteer work. I found the Office for Hispanic Affairs, a tiny Catholic Church–sponsored organization in the Fruitvale area of Oakland, and talked my way into a volunteer job supporting a lawyer and a paralegal who represented immigrant clients. I interviewed immigrants we were defending in their deportation proceedings and helped people fill out forms to bring in relatives and to become US citizens. This was my first exposure to immigration issues beyond my own family's experience, and I have been engaged in immigration policy ever since. Like many others in the immigration policy world, I don't think of myself as having chosen the issue. It feels as if it chose me.

I don't remember being aware of that at the time, though. I thought my volunteer work was interesting, but I didn't think it was leading me to my life's work. At twenty-two, I was pretty sure I wanted some kind of job at an organization that provided social services to needy people, and my volunteer gig gave me useful insight into what that might be like. I didn't really have a vision for what kind of services I was interested in providing, and I didn't intend to pursue a career in immigration. I suppose that if I had had that kind of clarity, I might have gone to law school. Instead, I was getting a degree in Latin American studies and diving into things that interested me like Chicano literature, while also learning about how immigration laws and policies affect people. I had no idea how important this would ultimately be.

My point is that there's value in what you learn in school and in what you learn in the course of your life. And if you are paying attention to what really interests you, the stuff that feels the least like work to you and more like something you want to be doing because it feels engaging, interesting, or important, the greater the likelihood that you are finding markers that will set you on your path. At least that's how it worked for me.

Discover What You're Good at, Even if It Means Failing Along the Way

They say that one learns a lot from failure. This adage has been true for me. In fact, the whole trajectory of my career began when I set a course for myself that turned out to be a terrible fit. When I was getting ready to leave graduate school, I was confident of two things. First, I wanted to be back in the Midwest, closer to home. California had opened my horizons, taught me a lot about myself, and connected me more closely to the Latinx community. But it also didn't feel like home, and the pull of home was strong for me. I wanted to be someplace where it would be easy to visit my parents and extended family.

My older sister had started her career in Chicago, which I knew to be a vibrant city only a four-hour drive or train ride from home. Chicago has an enormous Latinx population, so it seemed like a place where I might find work that would allow me to be of service in some way, which is the second thing I was sure of. I wasn't particular about what kind of work it was, as long as it connected to the Hispanic community and felt as if I was helping address challenges like the high school dropout rate, which was high at the time, or access to health care, which was low. I also had a boyfriend who had just gotten a job there, so the planets seemed to be aligning. Chicago it was.

Aside from the boyfriend and one friend from college (my sister had long-since relocated to Michigan), I knew absolutely nobody in Chicago. I perused the yellow pages (that's what we did before the Internet) looking for Latinx-focused social service agencies to introduce myself to. I had one letter of introduction from a graduate school friend, a priest who had contacts in the Catholic Archdiocese. Thanks to that letter, I found a job with Catholic Charities, the largest social service provider in the city, helping parishes in immigrant neighborhoods organize their own neighborhood-based social services. The pay was modest, but it was enough to cover the cost of living in a tiny studio apartment. The job met all my goals: Latinx-focused social services. Perfect.

Except that it didn't last long.

Two months after I started my new job, Congress passed a major immigration reform law that provided a one-year window for undocumented immigrants to come forward and apply to become legal residents, a process known as legalization. As it happened, Father Charles Rubey, the priest who oversaw my division at Catholic Charities—my boss's boss—was also the guy assigned to figure out how the Archdiocese was going mobilize to help immigrants get their legal status. Because of my brief bit of volunteer immigration experience, I had questions for him. Would he start a separate division and hire a team, or use the existing legal services office at Catholic Charities? Did Catholic Charities have enough bilingual personnel to handle the challenge? Were they coordinating with other service providers in the city?

I was worried that I was making a pest of myself, but these felt like important questions to me, and in my youthful zeal for the subject, I naively assumed that my supervisors were following the issues as closely as I was and coming up with answers. I was wrong about that; evidently, my tiny bit of background was more than anybody else at the agency had.

It never occurred to me to angle for a job as Father Rubey grappled with the task of designing Catholic Charities' approach to legalization. I had a job already, and I was only a few months in and still learning the ropes. So, I was surprised when one morning, my supervisor, Sister Rosemary Meyer, called me in to say that Father Rubey wanted to speak with me. She had a note in her voice that made it sound like something serious was happening, so I wondered whether I was in trouble. I walked into Father Rubey's office, where I sat in slack-jawed astonishment as he told me that the Lord had sent him a message in a dream. That message was that I should lead the legalization program for Catholic Charities.

I am not making this up.

The moral of the story for you is definitely not that you should wait for the good Lord to tell your future boss that s/he should hire you. Though I consider myself a person of faith, I don't believe that Father Rubey received a message from God; I believe that he was anxious about how he was going to get a legalization program up and running, and the pesky kid on Sister Rosemary's staff seemed to know stuff. So, he took a crazy chance on a twenty-four-year-old in her first job out of graduate school with zero management experience.

If I had had mentors at the time, I hope they would have told me that it was crazy to take that job and that any supervisor giving an employee that kind of responsibility on the basis of a dream or desperation is not exercising good judgment. But I had no mentors, I was in a new city, and I could see clearly enough that, inexperienced as I was, there was nobody else in that enormous organization who knew much about what was going on. I knew enough to know that the legalization period was a huge opportunity for millions of people, including tens of thousands in Chicago, and at that point we had only four months to set up a program. I believed that my path was to forge a career through which I could help the Latinx community. I was scared to death, but I took the job.

Setting up that program, running it, and doing the cleanup when the one-year legalization process was over was one of the scariest and most exhilarating times of my life. I built a team that set up offices in twelve parishes across two counties, with a total staff that peaked at thirty-five people. We helped form a coalition (now called the Illinois Coalition for Immigrant and Refugee Rights) with the other organizations in the city that were also working to legalize people, and we made sure we were collaborating rather than competing. In the end, this collaboration was hugely successful. We helped many thousands of people go from being undocumented to becoming legal permanent residents, and the program I was running was the largest of the bunch.

I learned so much from that experience. Lesson number one was that the kind of work that I thought I was destined to do—working in a program that provided a vital service to people in need, the kind of work that I think of as direct service—is not what I'm cut out for.

I discovered in those intense two years in Chicago that I just didn't have what it takes to be an effective direct service provider. As proud as I was of the positive results of our work for thousands of people, I couldn't let go of the fact that there were also many people that we couldn't help because they didn't qualify under the law. Worse, I couldn't let go of the faces of the people who didn't qualify. This was the late 1980s, the era depicted in the movie *Broadcast News*, which has a memorable scene in which the highly strung lead, played by Holly Hunter, manages the stress of her job by spending ten minutes every morning crying. That was me, except I mostly cried in the evening.

I agonized. I lost sleep. The scale at which we were able to help people didn't feel big enough, and the law seemed too restrictive. I spoke to a reporter about the part of the new law that was going to make it illegal for undocumented people to find work, describing my job as "like watching people be pushed off a cliff, knowing that you can save only a few of them." That was hardly the language of someone who is energized by what she is doing. I couldn't focus on being glad for the thousands we were helping. I was too busy worrying about those we couldn't help, and although I was doing my job effectively, it was taking a large emotional toll.

In the course of that work, I met many people who are good at managing the tension between what they can accomplish for people and what is beyond their grasp. There were social workers and other good people at Catholic Charities who confronted it every day as they served people struggling with poverty, substance abuse, and discrimination. They grieved and fought for those who fell through the cracks, managing to balance it all in their own hearts in order to get up and do it all again the next day. That's the kind of person I thought I was going to be. I was disappointed with myself when I discovered that I wasn't. I couldn't find that balance, and it became obvious to me that I wasn't likely to find it.

But even as I struggled with what I couldn't control, couldn't let go of, and wasn't good at in those years, I began to discover something else, too: I learned that I am a natural advocate. As I collaborated with the leaders of other programs like mine, we discovered that we were all answering anxious questions from families who feared coming forward to legalize. The rules weren't yet clear, so those seeking legal documentation couldn't possibly know whether getting a bag of food from the food pantry would count against them in the legalization process, or whether coming forward might jeopardize other family members who had arrived after the 1982 eligibility date and didn't qualify to legalize.

Because many of these families were nervous about coming forward themselves, and because we couldn't reassure them without clarity from the government, we concluded that part of our job was to act as their advocates and raise their questions and concerns with the government on their behalf. And when the government took steps that would harm families or undercut the purpose of the program, our job was to push back, also on their behalf. Because we were in contact every day with people en-countering obstacles to the very process intended to help them, we weren't just helping families through the mechanics of the legalization process but were also identifying important policy questions.

It was through this work that I discovered I was skilled at iden-tifying and explaining the problems and worries of the people who came through our doors for help. I turned out to be good at forming coalitions with others who were also serving the immi-grant community, so that there were a lot of organizations stand-ing together raising our voices on behalf of our clients. And I learned that I had a knack for building strategies to get problems fixed.

I started to get to know advocates working in Washington on the same problems at groups like the US Conference of Catho-lic Bishops, the National Council of La Raza, and the National Immigration Forum. Those organizations had relationships on Capitol Hill and in the executive branch, and those of us working directly with immigrants had information about what was work-ing and not working for them in the legalization process. To my astonishment, I learned that people I thought of as bigwigs in DC advocacy organizations didn't know everything. They needed to know what we were learning from our clients' struggles. We had information that they lacked. I learned how to describe real-world circumstances affecting real-world people in a way that others could understand and relate to, and I learned how to leverage this information into policy changes that could affect my clients' lives. I had found my calling as an advocate.

I'm telling you this story to highlight two things. First, the key to success is not the credentials that you build; it's about finding and doing the kind of work where your skills and your interests best align. I think of it as finding the work of your heart, because that's how I experienced it. For me, living with the reality that there were so many people that we couldn't help felt disempowering, but lifting their circumstances in the hope of making change felt completely different. It was as if I was using my particular set of skills for a purpose that might do some good. It felt like finding my voice.

Finding the work of my heart was about learning what kind of job best suited my ambitions for serving people in need. And it can be wonderful when doing the work of your heart is also how you make your living. But that's not the only way to express yourself in the world. The work of your heart is about engaging in something that feels like who you are, whether or not it's your paid job. That thing you're passionate about could be the thing that you do on the weekends, or the tutoring you do as a volunteer every Tuesday evening. The key is that it feeds you in some way.

The second important lesson from that experience is that it's okay to recognize when you aren't doing something well or when something about the role you have or the job you're in doesn't feel quite right, and to change course accordingly. Although it's accurate to say that I did not succeed in what I first set out to do for myself, which was to make a career of serving people directly, it's also true that being open to the possibility that I had made the wrong turn led me to find my footing in what would ultimately become my lifelong career. I am an advocate — I just didn't know it until I went to Chicago to do the work that I thought I was meant to do, and failed.

When You're Not Sure What You Want

Not everybody starts out with a clear sense of what they want to do. I came out of school with a few ideas (provide services in the Latinx community, live closer to home in the Midwest). Even if I ultimately changed course, at least I had some sense of direction to change course from. Not everybody has that, and not every job—especially an entry-level job—comes with the kinds of responsibilities that help you determine whether this is the work of your heart.

It's okay to find out through trial and error. Sometimes we choose a direction because we think it's something the world expects of us. Michelle Obama and Valerie Jarrett both write in their memoirs that they became lawyers because it seemed like a pathway to success. They had a picture in their heads of what their lives would be like, and when they got there, their lives fit that picture: they were earning a lot of money and working in fancy offices. But neither of them liked the actual work. Both ultimately chose less lucrative jobs in shabbier offices and were much happier as a result. That's the thing about picturing a job and the life that goes along with it before you're in it. You might like what it feels like, but then, you might not.

And even if you know what field you want to work in, sometimes (often) entry-level jobs are not the most interesting or engaging. Some people start out as assistants and interns, answering phones, making copies, and doing the things that the more experienced people have already moved away from. Sometimes you're bartending or waiting tables while looking for the opportunities that might lead to a career. Sometimes bartending and waiting tables *is* the career, providing you with a living while you spend time doing other things that you care about.

The key questions to ask yourself are: Am I happy? Am I learning? Am I around people who are doing jobs that look interesting, engaging, and useful? Are those jobs that I aspire to? Do I admire and respect the people who are doing them? Do I see a road to a job that I will like better? Does this job provide for me in a way that leaves me room for other things in my life that are important? A lot of us get meaning from our jobs. Many of us work to make it possible to do other things that give us meaning, whether it's raising a family, writing poetry, or indulging in a passion for skydiving. Ask yourself: If this isn't yet the life that I want, does it put me on a path to that life? Do I see a way to get there? Or am I learning what I don't want to do in the service of finding out what I do want?

Sometimes a job seems wonderful on paper because you're working on something you care about, but the environment is toxic for other reasons. You're teaching at the school where you always wanted to teach, but the principal is a disaster and everybody is miserable. Your team has a great assignment, but your teammates are at one another's throats. I had one of those. When my program was ending at Catholic Charities, I had a chance to shape the next phase of the organization's work to provide legal services to immigrants. The work felt important to me, but I had learned that it didn't make me happy, and I wasn't always comfortable with the fact that frequently less-qualified priests were in decision-making positions supervising often much better qualified women. What it looked like on the surface—meaningful and fulfilling—didn't match what it felt like to be in it. This was a situation that I couldn't fix, even though I was drawn to the picture of what that job looked like in my head. At the end of the day, it was important, but it wasn't the work of this particular heart. It's okay to focus on what's in your heart, even when a job looks pretty good on paper. And it's okay to let go of work that feels important if doing that work doesn't make you happy. In the end you will do the most good in the kind of work that fits with who you are so well that you forget sometimes that you're working.

Chapter 2

SHARP ELBOWS
AND OTHER TOOLS

I REACHED THE DECISION POINT ABOUT LEAVING THE WORK I was doing in Chicago after two years. The legalization initiative was concluding, and I had figured out that building the next phase of that work for Catholic Charities wasn't for me. So, I thought hard about what I had learned during my time there. I still had the same two goals: be of service to the Latinx community in some way, and live close to home in the Midwest. But I had also learned some things that helped me refine those goals. I had discovered that although I wasn't cut out for direct service, I felt at home as an advocate.

I had gotten to know a few people who worked for advocacy organizations in Washington, DC. I had met them maybe once or twice at meetings and had been on regular conference calls. They relied on the work of local service providers and advocates like me to keep them informed about how their work played out in the community. They seemed like good, smart people, doing the kind of advocacy work I had discovered I have an affinity for. But they were all in Washington. Was I willing to move?

I loved Chicago. I loved everything about it: the neighborhoods, the crazy politics, the lake—I even loved the winters. My relationship with my boyfriend had blown up, but even through heartbreak, I found new ways to make the city my own. I had made friends there, and it was close to my family in Michigan. I'm a Midwestern girl, and I felt at home. I had to think long and hard about whether I would consider a move to DC. In the end, I decided that I might be able to pull it off if I found the right job because I also had close friends there—people whom I had gone to college with. And it was still possible, though a little harder, to get home to Michigan when I needed to.

Moving was not a minor matter for me. I'm an introvert, comfortable with old friends, and not always at ease making new ones. Moving to a new city was a scary proposition, and I had already done it twice: once when I moved to California, and again to Chicago. I was ready to land in a place for good, and I thought Chicago was it. But the lure of potentially meaningful work was strong, and the fact that I had good friends in DC gave me the courage to consider it.

I took a deep breath and made a round of calls to the people I knew in DC, asking for their guidance as I searched for a new job.

My timing turned out to be excellent.

At the moment that I was thinking about my next steps, the National Council of La Raza (which we called NCLR; it has since changed its name to UnidosUS) was looking for middle managers. The organization was bouncing back from the devastating budget cuts of the Ronald Reagan administration, which had dramatically reduced government support for organizations working to address poverty and discrimination.

I was one of three new midlevel policy staffers, all Latinas and all twenty-six or twenty-seven years old. We joined a policy team that included other analysts working on education, health, and a range of other issues. The team was overwhelmingly female, except for our wonderful boss, Charles Kamasaki, who is brilliant, a little gruff, and exceptionally kind. Until my arrival, Charles had been responsible for the immigration work at NCLR, which meant that I had worked with him from my perch in Chicago. When I was looking to leave Catholic Charities, the first call I made was to Charles. I found out thirty years later that after I called, he went out of his way to cobble together the funding to hire me.

Much of the NCLR policy team's job was to tell the story of the Latinx community to policy makers in places like Congress, federal agencies like the Department of Education, and the media. We had all joined the organization just as the very first government data was emerging that could allow us to paint a picture of our own community, because the 1980 US Census was the first one to attempt to count Hispanics accurately. The Census, the constitutionally required, once-a-decade count of every person living in the United States, is important because it is the main source of data for everything we know about the United States and who we are. It tells us how well educated we are; our incomes; our family sizes; and our access to water, roads, and sanitation. If you are using Google to find out something about this country, chances are you are getting information that originates with the Census. At NCLR, we were using the Census to educate ourselves—and the people who make the laws that affect us—about who we are and what we as Latinx people need to succeed.

The NCLR I joined in 1988 was still very much focused on educating the rest of official Washington about our community's existence, as well as developing and promoting a fact-based set of policy goals to advance the country by advancing our community. I consider it one of the great privileges of my life to have arrived on the scene at a point at which we were moving from invisible to visible, from a community struggling to explain itself to a major political and economic force. What an exciting time to begin my life as a professional woman! During the time I worked at NCLR, Hispanic Americans became the largest minority in the United States, and we are still only beginning to realize our potential to shape our country.

Being Sharp, Outside and In

In the 1980s NCLR formally trained its staff to be especially watchful of typos in our documents because if there was a spelling error in a report or a funding proposal, we would be confirming the common assumption that Hispanic people lack full command of the English language. I was expected to dress professionally because, as we learned from the experience of the people who came before us, if our outward appearance was sloppy, people would question our professionalism. To be heard and respected as authorities about our *own* community, we needed to convey through what we said and how we looked that we were consummate professionals.

As a woman—and, let's be honest, a short woman (I am five feet two inches)—observing the norms when it came to "dressing for success" was especially important. That meant wearing structured clothes and nothing at all revealing; shoes with heels, to look professional (and to make me as tall as humanly possible); and pantyhose, even in the hot Washington summer—all to convey a sense of authority, if not power.

This may sound hopelessly old-fashioned, and it was. I share it because it reveals how hard we young Latinas worked in those days to meet and exceed traditional expectations of professionalism, precisely because at the time, Washington knew and thought so little about us, and expected even less. But as old-fashioned as pantyhose may sound to you today, I think there is a lesson here that still applies about the importance of how one presents oneself.

My friend Patricia Worthy is an eminent law school professor at Howard University, the most prominent of the nation's historically Black colleges and universities. She tells me that in the legal profession, the rules about dress haven't shifted much since she graduated from law school in 1969 and began to forge a career, becoming the first woman of color in almost every position she held. She still urges her law students to dress conservatively and professionally, and models this by doing so herself when she's teaching them. In her career, she felt that she had to present herself in a way that would be respected by her colleagues, and she believes strongly that this is still true for her students, who are largely African Americans looking to make their way in the legal profession. "I explain to my students that we still have to prove ourselves," she says. "They have a sense of freedom; they like to express who they are with their clothes, jewelry, and hair, but the profession is still conservative. Some kinds of jewelry won't work at a law firm."

Other women of color I spoke with agree with this approach. Tyra Mariani, an African American woman who is the president and COO of New America, a DC think tank where I also work, remembers that when she was in her twenties and looked younger than her age, she thought her looks detracted from her ability to be taken seriously, so she wore a lot of makeup to try to look more mature. She and Kathy Ko Chin, the petite, dynamic leader of the Asian & Pacific Islander American Health Forum, agree with me that being short is also a thing that can prevent us from being taken seriously. We have all compensated for it in the same way, too, by wearing suits and heels. Kathy even wore a suit and heels as a college student.

Patricia Worthy tells an amazing story about once having to wage a court battle over what she wore. This was in the 1970s, when women were still expected to wear skirts and dresses, especially in a professional setting. (I was still in grade school then, but I remember distinctly that we were not allowed to wear pants to school, even in the cold Michigan winters, except that we were permitted to wear them under our skirts on days when we had gym class.) Patricia's story says a lot about how hard women had to fight for the wardrobe flexibility that we have:

> When I started practicing law, there weren't a lot of women practicing in DC. Very few of us were litigators in court, trying cases. When the pantsuit came into fashion, I went to the chief of the DC Superior court, wearing a pantsuit, and asked if it would be inappropriate to wear a pantsuit to the court. I got approval for a pantsuit. It had to be a suit: pants with a matching jacket, not just a blouse. One time, I was trying a case in federal district court and I got a call for an unscheduled status hearing. The judge went berserk because I had a pantsuit on. He was "shocked and dismayed" at what I was wearing. I said, "Your Honor, this wasn't scheduled, so I came dressed as I am. I have never known there to be a dress code for the district court." He said, "There is one for my courtroom." I asked him, "Can you tell me what it is?" He responded, "Look around you." So I did. I looked around me and I saw white guys with pinstripe suits on. So, I got my seamstress to make a three-piece pinstripe suit. I got a man's shirt and tie; I got a watch with a gold chain. He had me arrested for contempt of court. The marshals carried me out of the courtroom to a cellblock downstairs. I was down there playing cards with the guards and my partners came and got me. I appealed the judge's ruling. I knew I had him, because I had followed his instructions to the letter. He apologized in open court. His wife and other women had stopped speaking to him because he had me arrested. I was the talk of the town.

I love this story, not just because it shows the kind of courage Patricia and women like her have had to show to establish our professional credibility but also because it shows the kind of courage we sometimes have to exhibit just to be ourselves.

Patricia's story isn't just an illustration of ancient history. Many of us still grapple with how to present ourselves in ways that feel true to who we are and that are also appropriate to the settings in which we live and work. Pramila Jayapal, who was a Seattle-based advocate for vulnerable immigrants when we first met, tells me that while she hates to admit it, her insecurities and doubts arise most frequently when it comes to figuring out how to dress for her job. Granted, her job is in a pretty rarified setting: Pramila is the first woman of South Asian heritage to serve in the US Congress. But her experience isn't that different from Patricia's students preparing to work in law firms. It can be a challenge to figure out how to be you and also convey what's expected in your role.

"I feel like we're supposed to wear certain things, and they're not really me, and I don't really know how to do it," she tells me. She stays away from wearing traditional clothes from India when she does events, even at home in Seattle, because she worries that people might not want to be in photos with her wearing something that exotic. She tries to find small ways to express and highlight who she is, because it feels important to her: "I do it with the colors that I wear, jewelry that is ethnic in flavor—nothing too overstated. It's an area where I have some work to do."

I wish I could say that the time for having to worry about these things has passed, but I don't think that's the case. I can say that after thirty years as a professional, I don't think about conveying authority through my clothing as much as I used to. I have reached a point in my career where I am capable of being authoritative even when my short self is in a pair of jeans and flats. But the context matters. If I were to walk into the West Wing again to offer guidance on a policy issue, you would likely find me in heels and a dress.

I am also acutely aware that there are other, perhaps more important ways to convey authority than what I wear. I still cultivate a sense of being sharp and on my game—the thing that my clothes were meant to convey when I was in my twenties—by being prepared, knowing my subject matter well enough to sound and be authoritative, and conveying enthusiasm because I am passionate about what I do. Every woman of color I spoke to while preparing this book said she does the same.

I don't try to be taller than I am anymore, but I do try to take up space in the room in other ways. It's worth thinking about what people see when you walk into the room: Do they see someone who takes the time to be prepared, or someone who doubts herself? Do they see someone who believes that her experience will contribute to a quality discussion, or someone who lacks confidence?

The most important element in how you present yourself, of course, is not your clothes, but your preparation, your self-confidence, and the sense that you know that what you bring into the room is valuable. But it is also true that what you wear will make an impression. It will communicate something about you to the people in the room and perhaps even to yourself. So, what do you want to communicate? The more deliberate you are about conveying who you want to be in that room, the more people will see you and what you bring.

Getting Coached and Being Sharp
(Only Occasionally with Actual Elbows)

I didn't have much in the way of role models or mentors until I got to Washington and started work at NCLR. If I were giving advice to twenty-something me, I would suggest seeking them out—finding people I admire, especially women, to provide some guidance and advice. Fortunately for me, I had stumbled into a situation in which my boss, Charles Kamasaki, was an excellent and thoughtful guide; he was gruff on the outside, but not enough to hide the heart of gold that guides him.

Charles passed along some of the lessons he learned from our mutual boss, Raul Yzaguirre, whose fearless leadership had saved the organization from the blow of the Reagan budget cuts, and who was determined for Hispanic Americans to assume what he saw as our rightful place in shaping the destiny of the country. It mattered to Raul that we dress professionally to project our professionalism and ambitions for the community, and Charles made that clear to his team. And he coached me in other ways that I remember with great fondness and gratitude.

Like me, Charles is not a tall person. But unlike me, he had the knowledge, confidence, and swagger to fill up the room and hold his own with the guys in the DC immigration world, who had formed something of a brotherhood working together to pass the Immigration Reform and Control Act of 1986. There were women in the circle, too, but when I got to DC, the clear breakdown of roles was that the men were the ones who devised legislative strategy, worked with Congress, and took calls from the media, and the women were more likely to be behind the scenes, focused on implementation of the new law. Charles hired me to assume *his* role in this family of advocates when I came to Washington, and he helped me do it by all but disappearing from every table and meeting that he typically attended. My new colleagues had no choice but to accept my presence in the circle, though some resisted it for what felt like a long time.

Among the more memorable examples of Charles's coaching was the time he taught me how to literally elbow my way into a circle of tall men. Part of my job was to go to the congressional hearings on immigration issues, where the usual gang (mostly guys) would attend, have all-important side conversations with congressional staff around the margins of the hearing, and gather to strategize when the hearing was over. This strategizing often took place in a literal huddle; they would stand together in a circle to compare notes from their various conversations and plot out their next moves.

I was missing vital information because I couldn't break my way into their circle, both literally and figuratively. I complained to Charles; it was clear to me that if he had been there, he would have been in that circle, and it didn't seem fair that I was excluded. Charles was very matter of fact. He said, "Look, you're short, you're new, you're younger than they are, and you're a woman. They're not being deliberately rude; they're just not used to including you. So, use your elbow like this and say, 'Hey, guys, can you make a little room for a colleague, here?'" It was excellent advice, and once it was clear that I was willing to elbow my way in, I never had to use a literal elbow again.

I confess, however, that during my adjustment to the ways of Washington, in order to convey the toughness that my physical presence did not, I took up swearing. This is not something I am particularly proud of and it is not something I recommend to you, either. If I am being honest, I have to admit that I cultivated cursing as a habit because I felt that it helped me fit in and compensated for what everybody was seeing: a short, unassuming Hispanic woman, not exactly tough-looking, even in a suit and heels. All of the guys sprinkled their language with epithets pretty much all the time, and while it didn't come as naturally to me, I remember being deliberate about adding a few colorful words and expressions to my vocabulary, thinking salty language would give me some credibility in the boys' club that I was trying to break into.

Being comfortable swearing came in handy during my years at the White House, where it again felt like an asset, a sign of toughness. Even into my forties and fifties, I was still compensating for being short and soft-spoken. I left the White House at the end of the Obama administration for a less intense professional atmosphere, and for the first time in thirty years, aware of being more comfortable in my own skin, I find myself tapering off this habit.

In retrospect, I see that I picked up swearing as kind of a shortcut, a quick pathway to acceptance into the club that I felt excluded from. Assuming male patterns of behavior and leadership—including those that don't come naturally—is a strategy that lots of women adopt to get the job done. Our images of leadership have been predominantly male, so we adopt that model of presenting ourselves. Our work uniforms were suits, modeled after what professional men wore, but with bows on our blouses. We adopted external markers to show that we could succeed as we edged our way into male-dominated fields.

I see signs all around me that those days are ending, though it is not happening nearly fast enough. It makes me proud (and relieved) to see women recognizing that the best way to show our abilities and leadership qualities is to be ourselves. The rules are steadily changing as we bring our own approaches to leadership, and there's less of a sense that we must be one of the guys if we expect to lead.

But it's still true that there are too few women overall in visible leadership positions in places like Congress or corporate leadership, and there are *way* too few women of color. My former White House colleague Valerie Jarrett likes to say, "It's hard to be what you can't see" as she encourages women and girls of color to blaze new trails and see themselves in positions that have rarely, if ever, been occupied by women. Too many of us are still the first people who look like us in our respective jobs and positions, and there are still many trails that have yet to be blazed.

Suit-clad, high-heeled me may have had to use actual elbows thirty years ago, and those elbows may still be necessary from time to time. But I have hope that we are making inroads, that many of us no longer must pretend to be taller, or male, or white in order to assert our ability to make an impact in our work or to lead the charge. We are beginning to have role models who look like us, who are not afraid to bring their full selves to the task at hand, and who recognize that we will get farther if we have a diversity of voices in the room. The purpose of a role model is to point the way and show what is possible. The rest is up to you.

Remember to Value What You Know

When I was younger, demonstrating confidence that what I knew from my own experience and perspective had value did not come easily. I've learned by talking to other women, especially women of color, that I am not the only one. Many of us are cautious in new situations and automatically assume that the more experienced people around us have lots and lots of knowledge that we don't have. For my part, I tend to hold back until I either feel comfortable that my assumption is incorrect or have ascertained that I am as well-grounded in the subject as I need to be.

Most of the time, this is a good instinct. There are few things worse than a newcomer who thinks they know everything when they clearly don't. But it also means that I tend to start with an assumption that what I bring to the conversation, based on my experience and my expertise, isn't nearly as valuable as the stuff that the people around me bring.

If I were giving advice to my younger self, I would advise myself to remember to value my experience as a Latina, a daughter of an immigrant family, and a person with expertise that comes from being part of and working with the community that I sought to represent. I would tell my younger self that however dazzled I might be by the policy expertise and "inside-the-beltway" experience of the people around me when I got to Washington, those people also needed to know what I knew from my work in Chicago and my experience as a human being walking through this world.

One example is that moment early in my career when Charles, my NCLR boss, stepped away from the various coalition tables, leaving me to take his place, even as he was watching out for me behind the scenes. Some of my colleagues were unhappy about that, and one even confronted me directly. Reacting to my presence at his board meeting in place of Charles, he asked me, "Does your presence here mean that NCLR is reducing its commitment to my organization?"

I remember being taken aback by the question, and clearly it made an impression on me because I still remember it thirty years later. But I don't remember what I said, or whether I said anything at all. What I wish I had been able to draw upon at the time is the advice I frequently give my younger colleagues, which is to remember that we bring experience and expertise to the table by virtue of who we are—that experience matters. Especially when we are the onlies in the room, which still happens all the time to people of color in these kinds of settings, we know things that the rest of the room doesn't know. And to do the work well, those people need to recognize what we bring. That's a major reason that having diversity in the room matters.

In my case, for example, while I had plenty still to learn from the people in the room, I also had knowledge about the people I had just been serving in Chicago. I knew about how the immigration system worked from the point of view of the immigrant community, and I was one of the few people in the room with that knowledge. I was the only woman, the only Latinx. But I didn't fully recognize or value what I knew, and I wasn't able to express why others should value it, either. Now, I would tell my twenty-something self to walk into that room with the calm confidence that, for all their experience, none of the men in that room brought what I brought to the work. That would have made it easier to say what I didn't say: "My organization sent me because I know what I'm doing. Now, let's get on with it."

This doesn't apply only to someone like me who was doing work explicitly focused on my community, where it's more obvious that my expertise mattered. Plenty of us are firsts and onlies at the tables we sit at, whether we work in the human resources department or on an engineering team solving a technical problem, and there are plenty of ways in which our lived experience matters to a team's ability to get the job done well. And frankly, even if you aren't a first or an only, many of the workplaces where we find ourselves are places where either we're underrepresented or the people we work with really don't know what we know. We're in professions—teaching, nursing, social work, journalism or publishing, arts and fashion, or advertising and marketing— where our expertise is directly relevant to the people we're serving, or for whom we're designing products or services. The world needs more of what we bring to it, no matter where we are, and it's important to remind yourself of that.

Honestly, this is a lesson that I keep relearning. No matter how much confidence I've gained, there will be new situations, people, roles, and challenges to confront, in which I will again be a beginner. I can still experience that uncertainty, even after thirty years. But if that weren't the case, it would mean I'd stopped learning and growing. And I have learned over time to continually remind myself that the experience and expertise I bring has value.

Much more recently, in my last year at the White House, I found myself again having to dig deep and remember that I brought knowledge and experience to a room of extraordinary people who, for all of their smarts and expertise, didn't have my particular lens or vantage point. This was in the early days of Donald Trump's candidacy for president, before official Washington took him seriously. No one I worked with believed he would survive the Republican primaries, let alone win the election of 2016. The conventional wisdom among Democrats when he entered the race was amazement and even glee because the Republicans were embroiled in a nasty primary fight, and it seemed obvious that letting them tear one another apart could only weaken the eventual Republican candidate, to the benefit of his Democratic opponent, who everyone assumed would be Hillary Clinton.

I was frequently in the room with people who had made this calculation, people who were on President Obama's senior team and who met every morning to discuss the challenges of the day. When we reached the point in the discussion about whether President Obama should respond to any of the uglier statements that Trump made as he was campaigning—remember that he famously launched his campaign by calling Mexican immigrants "rapists"—the conventional wisdom was that the president should say nothing and let the Republicans eat one another alive. I wasn't comfortable with this logic, though I understood it. I pointed out what was obvious to everybody, which is that Trump's comments were over the top and offensive, but that wasn't necessarily enough for the leader of the free world to make a public statement in response. Yet I remained uneasy and found myself unable to articulate why. A part of me thought that maybe I should just leave the political judgments to the political experts—after all, my expertise is not politics but public policy.

I thought about this hard over the course of several weeks, frustrated with the feeling that there was more to be said, but unable to find the words to explain why I thought we were missing something important. Finally, I did what I often did when I was struggling with something, which was to find my way to Valerie

Jarrett's office to ask her advice. She listened and helped me road test a couple of lines of argument to help me see what I was missing, but most of all, she affirmed the thing that I had begun to doubt, which is that I had a perspective to offer to the president's other advisors and that I saw something by virtue of my experience that they might not see.

Thanks to Valerie's intervention, I was finally able to explain that my discomfort was about the fact that Trump's harmful, over-the-top words weren't just offensive on their face; they gave legitimacy to similar hostile and racist feelings held by others, and this, as history shows us, often leads to real outcomes that harm actual people. We now have evidence that this is exactly what happened in this case: increases in hate crimes and harassment against immigrants, Muslims, and others who were the subject of Trump's verbal attacks during the campaign and since. But in the early days, this wasn't so obvious, and it wasn't easy to explain.

Valerie said another wise thing when I sought her out for help. She said that although it was important to do my best to explain my point about Trump's startling statements in a way that my colleagues would understand, I wouldn't have to persuade President Obama that he needed to get out there in public to respond. "He is going to get asked, and you and I both know that we don't have to worry about the answer," Valerie said. She was, of course, right about that.

Don't Be Afraid to Ask for Help, and Remember to Pay It Forward

As I look back on my early years in Chicago and DC, I realize that it never occurred to me to network, find a mentor, or even ask for help, which was a mistake. I didn't have much in the way of role models, especially female ones. In fact, I don't remember meeting a single woman of color in a position of authority during my years in graduate school or in Chicago. Not one. I hope this has changed as far as you're concerned, and that you have more to choose from in the way of mentors and guides. It's important to build a circle of peers that you can trust, and to be brave enough to seek out people you admire to ask for guidance from time to time.

I had no idea. I did none of this. Now that I look back, I see that I was very, very lucky. My boss Charles Kamaski was my most influential mentor without my ever asking, and there were many other people helping me make my way, whose support I didn't fully recognize or understand at the time.

They're out there for you, too, though you're more likely to find them if you're looking.

My first coach was a Chicago priest who had no earthly reason to support me other than the fact that he was a big-hearted, generous man. I was fresh out of graduate school and brand new to Chicago, and I'd arrived without a job and with exactly one useful connection thanks to a graduate school classmate, a Holy Cross father named Tim Scully who is now a major figure at Notre Dame. Father Tim barely knew me, and I never would have dreamed of asking him for help, but out of simple generosity he offered to write me a letter of introduction to a priest he knew in Chicago. I had no idea that his priest friend was the very eminent Monsignor John J. Egan, who is revered in Chicago as a champion for social justice.

Monsignor Egan had participated in Dr. Martin Luther King Jr.'s groundbreaking march from Selma to Montgomery and had led the Archdiocesan Office of Urban Affairs in the 1950s and '60s, fighting urban segregation with passion and principle. I am still in awe that he bothered with a very young me. Father Jack (he never let me call him "Monsignor") taught me more about mentoring than anybody I have ever known, before or since. He met with me because of Father Tim's letter, and arranged for me to meet the nun who was the head of personnel for Catholic Charities, who promptly set me up with a job interview that landed me my first job. That small act of kindness on Father Tim's part had a huge impact on my life.

But Father Jack's support didn't stop there. He met with me regularly, several times a year, taking me out for meals and coaching me through the many challenges of doing the work, even as I was discovering that I wasn't cut out for my intended role as a service provider. Even after I moved to Washington, he kept in touch, looking me up when he was in town and taking me out for long breakfasts where he continued to offer me gentle wisdom and precious guidance. He showed me that no matter how important people think you are, it's important to make room for simple kindness and look for leadership in the people who cross your path, no matter how young and inexperienced they are or how little you know about them. He was put in my path by the thoughtfulness of an acquaintance, by providence, or maybe by luck, but I remember him every time a young colleague asks for support, and I attempt to do for that person what Father Jack did for me.

Sometimes coaches are people who take the time to point out something that you might be missing, something that they spot while you're working together on something else. That's how Wade Henderson influenced me in my first months in DC. He was one of the guys from that group of guys that I elbowed my way into when I first got to DC. At the time, he was the deputy director of the Washington office of the American Civil Liberties Union (ACLU). Wade would go on to be the Washington representative for the NAACP and then lead the Leadership Conference on Civil Rights, becoming something of a civil rights legend in Washington. I don't remember being aware of it at the time, but he put a lot of effort into supporting young people of color who were starting their careers, and into coaching their older, more experienced colleagues in how to support them as well. I am lucky to say that I was one of the beneficiaries of his generosity. There are legions of us.

I remember Wade's coaching from my first-ever meeting of the executive committee of the National Immigration Forum, an organization that supported groups around the country working on behalf of immigrants and refugees. I had never sat on a board of directors before, let alone the executive committee. I was the only woman, the only Latinx, and a good decade younger than any of the guys in the room. Suit-wearing, new-to-swearing me, still learning the ropes and finding ways to seem authoritative, was intimidated, trying to figure out this new role and keeping quiet.

The committee members were used to having my boss, Charles, in the room. It wasn't yet clear to them that he was stepping away and putting me forward as his replacement. He hadn't told them, and it hadn't even fully dawned on me that that's what he was doing. Wade spotted my dilemma before I did and pulled me aside during the meeting, gently saying, "So maybe you need to do some truth in advertising. You're representing your organization on this board, not Charles. I think you should say so." I hadn't fully grasped that I was in a situation in which, if I expected to have a voice or convey any kind of authority as a full participant in the work, I was going to have to claim it. Out loud. It was a bit of a sink-or-swim situation, and Wade discreetly showed me how to paddle and keep myself afloat. Nobody else in the room would have done that for me if Wade hadn't been there.

Years later, one of the moments in which I knew that I had established myself was when Wade admonished me about not being generous enough to a male coalition partner whose work I thought wasn't up to par. He said something like, "Do you think there are so many Latino men at the table that we can afford not to support this one? Maybe you should be working on helping him succeed." He reminded me that my job wasn't just about getting to an outcome but also about supporting my colleagues so that we would get there together and all own the result. He was signaling that I was positioned to lead, and that leadership means lifting your colleagues and making it possible for them to succeed. I never forgot that lesson or Wade's generosity in offering it.

I think it's notable and important that so many of my early coaches were men. To me, this fact illustrates two things. First, although I have plenty of stories to tell about men in the policy world and in the White House who could be challenging to work with, I also had the good fortune to work with male colleagues whose thoughtfulness helped shape who I have become.

Second, I think it shows the extent to which I was operating in what was very much a man's world—both in the Catholic Church in Chicago, and in Washington. I have gotten incredible support from female colleagues, particularly in my later years at NCLR and in the White House. But frankly, there simply weren't as many women in a position to act as coaches and mentors to me back then because there weren't many women doing this work— especially not women of color.

Patricia Worthy says the same thing. As she attended law school in the 1960s and launched her career in the 1970s, she had many mentors and one hundred percent of them were white men. "My family didn't have friends who could mentor me," she says. "There was nobody in my world in a position to help me. The people who helped me were my teachers. They came to my parents to encourage me to go to the good high school. A Jewish professor at Brooklyn College took me aside and recommended that I go to law school. He told me, 'There are places where they won't let Black people take the LSAT law school entrance exam, but Howard University doesn't require it.' He paid for me to come to Howard on a bus. He had spoken to the dean of admissions, who was also a city university graduate. Not only did they admit me, but they gave me a full scholarship and a job as a research assistant. All of the people who helped me were white males."

Like me, Patricia didn't really think to ask for help. People stepped forward for her because they saw something in her and because they were generous. I think many people who are positioned to offer help are eager to do so, even if they don't take the initiative. It helps if you ask.

Even though my early Washington experience was dominated by men, I was fortunate that two white women were also watching out for me without my realizing it, the very first year that I got to DC. Jane O'Grady was a legendary lobbyist for the AFL-CIO (American Federation of Labor and Congress of Industrial Organizations), known for her strategic judgment and for being one of the few women on the team who got the Civil Rights Act passed in 1964. She led "O'Grady's Raiders," who did everything they could for precious congressional votes, including baking cookies for recalcitrant congressmen. She attended immigration hearings with Janet Kohn, a talented lawyer who had been one of the few women in her law school and who had an encyclopedic mind for policy.

Jane and Janet were in the room the very first time I testified before a congressional committee, which was a terrifying experience. I found out much later that when they left the hearing, they called my boss to tell him I had done a "magnificent" job. I don't remember being magnificent; I just remember getting through it. But I now understand that they were going out of their way to send a signal to my boss that I could do this thing, and they were watching out for me.

When I learned about what they had done, well after the fact, it taught me something important: Jane and Janet, who had blazed trails all by themselves, were trying to make my path a little easier. They taught me to be deliberate about supporting my colleagues—particularly women, and particularly people of color—and to pay attention to the younger ones whose bosses may not be there in the room to see them shine. Taking the time to put in a good word with the boss or send a note of encouragement, especially when a younger colleague is facing a challenge, can have an enormous impact.

You don't have to be at an advanced stage in your career to help someone else in theirs. Words of encouragement and support are valuable at any stage, from anyone who means them. If you foster an atmosphere in which you are cheering others on and lifting their work for others around them to see, you may well find that you're building the kind of positive collaboration and partnership with your colleagues that will help all of you shine brighter.

My former colleague Manar Waheed, a brilliant lawyer from a Pakistani Muslim family who worked on my immigration team at the White House, reinforced the importance of this lesson for me. As the Obama administration was coming to an end and we were all beginning to look for new jobs, I called a friend at the ACLU to tell him how wonderful Manar is. He did the smart thing and hired her, which seemed to me to be an obvious thing to do. Afterwards, Manar told me that every time she has gotten a new job or a promotion, it started with another woman of color making a call or going out of her way to open a door.

Every single time. What a wonderful thing to hear, that there are others who are doing their part to open the way for those coming up after us. There's always room to step up and add your voice to the chorus.

An experience Tyra Mariani had when she was in a very senior position at the Department of Education in the Obama administration underscored for her just how much women of color need one another in the workplace. She recalls being perplexed that women from around the agency seemed to find their way to her door with issues and questions. She remembers thinking, "Why are they coming to me?" Then she realized that she was one of only two senior women at the department, one of very few leaders who were people of color, and she understood that her presence sent a strong signal, one important enough that her colleagues were beating a path to her door.

Now, as president and COO of New America, the Washington think and action tank where I work, Tyra remembers that experience and makes a special effort to be a visible, welcoming presence to her colleagues who might be feeling unseen or unheard. She notices coworkers who sometimes feel invisible to or devalued by others: the security guard at the entrance to the building, the custodial staff who keep the offices sparkling, the hardworking people on the accounting staff, and the receptionist who answers the phones and greets every person who walks in the door. These colleagues are often women of color, and they are critical to the rest of the organization, even if they aren't always in a public-facing role. They know Tyra, that she's a leader of the organization, and that she knows and values them.

Around the moment when the Black Lives Matter movement was created, when protesters were mobilizing against police violence in Ferguson, Missouri, Tyra's work took her to Detroit, where she remembers a woman saying to her, "I feel my blackness every day all the time." It's a familiar feeling to Tyra. "You carry the weight of the identities that people can see and the underestimation that comes with that," she says. "I bought the T-shirt that has the word 'underrepresented' crossed out, followed by the word 'underestimated.' It's a theme for many underrepresented people."

Her explicit purpose in wearing that T-shirt to work is to make a statement for all her colleagues to see, and to make room for the people who see those words and know that she feels the same way they do. She sometimes wears an African mud cloth skirt to work for the same reason. It says something about who she is, and it sends a message that there's room for others to be who they are as well. As a leader, she is creating space for others who may not feel seen or heard.

Tyra is in a senior role at New America, and she's being deliberate about using that leadership to create a better atmosphere for others. You can do this, too, in subtler ways, even when you're not the president and COO. You do it by lifting your colleagues when they make a good point in a meeting and by being the person who goes out of her way to give a shout out when someone reaches a milestone or accomplishes a goal.

Although you can offer help to the people around you at any stage of your career, it may be a while before you have the seniority and the contacts to offer material help to others. But someday, the person in a position to be helpful with those just starting their careers will be you, and it will happen sooner than you think. Be aware of who is standing up for you now and reflect on how their help and support is useful to you. Can you be that person for someone else? Think about gathering your peers and creating spaces where you can support one another. That's what it means to pay attention and pay it forward. Be the person who makes it possible for the people coming up around you to have the support that you hope to have.

Chapter 3

DEALING WITH DOUBT
FROM OUTSIDE AND WITHIN

AFTER TWENTY FULFILLING YEARS AT NCLR I DID SOMETHING that I never thought I would do: I left to take a job in the US government. President Barack Obama had been elected in the fall of 2008, and though I had supported his campaign, I hadn't been thinking about trying to work for him. To my astonishment, he offered me a job on his senior team at the White House out of the blue, and when I hesitated, he insisted. So, in January of 2009, the day after his inauguration, I found myself in the surprising—and somewhat terrifying—position of walking into the West Wing for what would become the toughest and most inspiring eight years of my life. NCLR had prepared me in many ways for the challenges of those years in the West Wing, but I would also be tested in ways that were new to me. Sometimes this meant proving myself to the people around me, and sometimes my biggest challenge was overcoming my own doubts.

The president was straight with me about why he wanted me on board: I had briefed him many times on immigration issues while he was in the Senate, so he knew me as an immigration expert with deep ties in and knowledge of the Latinx community. He very much wanted to pass an immigration reform bill as president, and that's why he wanted me on the team. That was clear to me.

But it was also clear that nobody on his senior team knew me well. In fact, I had barely met any of them. It seemed to me that they rushed the announcement that I was joining the team, which happened only a few weeks after he was elected, to send a message that he had hired a senior-level Latina. So, although I was confident—if astonished—that the president thought highly of me and invited me in because of who I am and what I do, I wasn't so confident that the rest of the team knew much about me. On one hand, I thought they would be inclined to give me the benefit of the doubt; the president clearly thought I was worth bringing on board, and that's one heck of a recommendation. On the other hand, I knew that some of my new colleagues, who had never worked with me before, might see me as just a person who checked the Latinx box. They might have doubts about me. And it's not a big distance to go from wondering about their doubts to having a few myself.

Run the Race

I come by that sense of doubt honestly. One burden for women of color, no matter what our jobs, is that we often feel that we are fighting against the headwinds of some people's low expectations. Our challenge is compounded; we not only have to be on top of things, competent, and hardworking, but we frequently must prove that we are those things to people who don't start out being inclined to believe it. We are tested, whether we are ready or not. This can be true in almost every setting, even when you're working for the first African American president of the United

States, surrounded by people who believe in him and in his vision for a diverse government better serving a diverse country.

Supreme Court Justice Sonia Sotomayor talks eloquently about this phenomenon in her discussion of affirmative action in her memoir, *My Beloved World*. The push for diversity in college admissions got her to the starting line in a race she didn't even know she was running. That's how she went from the Bronx to Princeton. But she wasn't going to succeed just because she made it to the starting line. Showing up at Princeton was no guarantee that she was going to succeed. She still had to run the race. That was true when she got to college, and it was true when she was facing a panel of senators considering her nomination for the Supreme Court. There are always those who look at a woman of color and wonder whether she's qualified, or whether she's only there because of her ethnicity.

Frankly, in the years since Justice Sotomayor went to Princeton, it hasn't gotten much easier getting to the starting line. Deesha Dyer is an African American woman whose unconventional career started in her native Philadelphia, where she chronicled the hip-hop movement while also doing clerical work to make ends meet. She remembers hitting those low expectations early on: "I was working as a secretary," she explains, "and I remember wanting to do more. I said to them, 'I am thankful for my job, but really I am capable of doing more, like leading a team or taking some management courses.' I applied for a management skills workshop in the company and I got denied because, as they said, 'you're just a secretary. This is for leadership of this company.'"

Deesha asked her employer what kinds of classes she could take, and "they encouraged me to take Excel and Word—things I already knew. There's nothing wrong with being a secretary, but I just remember feeling so low and so angry because they were so sure that I was not management material. That hurt because all the people working as secretaries in the organization were Black, and they basically told all of us that."

Deesha wasn't being tested to see whether she could run the race; she was being dismissed without a chance at the starting line. She took her disappointment and anger straight to community college, to a White House internship, and ultimately to a huge job in the White House East Wing working directly for Michelle Obama. She got herself to the starting line, ran the race, and proved what she could do, not just to her colleagues but, more importantly, to herself.

Tyra Mariani has a similar story. When she was in her early twenties, she was a business analyst in an entry-level role at a major consulting firm. These are the kinds of roles that expand the skills of young professionals, but also serve as tryouts for more-permanent roles at the firm. But Tyra's tryout ended before she'd even gotten started.

"I was not extended an offer to return," she told me. "The partner told me that it wasn't clear to them that I was partner material. I was twenty-three. There are literally three or four different roles after graduate school that happen before you can become a partner. They evaluated my potential when I was twenty-three, before business school, and before I could fully show what I could do. I took a bullet to my confidence that it took me years to recover from. Years."

Looking back, Tyra believes that if she had had a cohort of people to process this feedback with, they might have helped her see how unreasonable it was for her bosses to assess her lifelong career potential in this way. Instead, she questioned herself, even as her career continued to progress, taking her from Stanford Graduate School of Business to becoming budget director for Chicago Public Schools and executive director of New Leaders for New Schools. "I kept thinking what I had achieved was due to some combo of preparedness, competence/skill, and luck, with luck comprising a big portion of the mix," Tyra says. "I've now been around long enough to know that opportunity, not luck, is a portion of the mix—but not the most significant for me, certainly not as a woman of color. That competence is the largest part of the pie. I wish my younger self had known that. I wonder what I could have done if I'd recognized I deserved to be in the rooms I was in and wasn't there by chance."

Those who underestimate the prodigious talents of people like Deesha and Tyra aren't just doing an injustice to gifted women but are also depriving their companies and organizations of the talent that they need to thrive. Study after study shows that diversity in the workplace is more than simply a goal to accomplish a social good or provide redress for discrimination that has held us back for generations. It's a strategy for a more successful workplace.

The evidence is widespread. A 2015 *McKinsey Quarterly* report on 366 public companies found that those with the most racial and ethnic diversity among their managers had better financial returns. So did those that were the most diverse by gender. *Harvard Business Review* finds that teams that reflect our nation's diversity are smarter than those that don't. They process facts more carefully and are more likely to find innovative solutions to problems. In 2017, *Forbes* magazine covered a study of 200 different business teams that found that diverse teams made better decisions 87 percent of the time, and they made those better decisions twice as fast as teams that weren't diverse.

It stands to reason that attracting talent from a diversity of backgrounds leads to better decision-making. It means that you have more perspectives in the room and more access to seeing an issue from a variety of angles. You shouldn't think of this finding just as evidence for someone else to see how valuable it is to have you on their team; it's something for you to remember in moments of doubt. Even if you're the only person like you in the room, everybody else benefits from you being there. They may know it or they may not, but they need what you bring.

When People Assume
You're Only There for a Little Color

I had an experience like Tyra's "we don't see you as partner material" episode when I worked in the White House. It was clear to me that some small number of my colleagues saw me as a person who owed my position to my ethnicity and didn't take seriously what I brought to the job. At least one colleague—a major one—implied this to a couple of journalists writing books. This is how I know I'm not making it up.

I am referring to Bill Daley, who was the third chief of staff of the five whom I served under in the White House. I had much less contact with Bill than I did with any of the others because his work style was very hierarchical and he spent much of his time with the most senior team. During most of his twelve-month tenure, I was on the next level of senior staff, which meant that my boss, Valerie Jarrett, was in the small 7:30 a.m. meeting, and I joined her in the larger 8:30 senior staff meeting every morning. I saw Bill every day, but we didn't work together closely. He was always polite, and I will always be grateful to him for the decent thing he did on the day when the *Washington Post* ran a story in 2011 titled "Activists Say Obama Aide Cecilia Munoz Has 'Turned Her Back' on Fellow Hispanics." I was traveling that day and he called me early in the morning to offer some encouragement: "Don't let it get to you. My father used to say, 'there's a reason they line birdcages with newspapers.'" It was a kind gesture.

But if I were to name the people who I wished would have taken me more seriously, and who I feared saw me as the Latina who was "there for diversity" and therefore less able to contribute compared to other members of the team, Bill would be high on that list. He never got to know me well, and under his leadership I had to fight more than usual to be included in meetings that directly related to my job.

During most of his tenure, I was the director of Intergovernmental Affairs, responsible for the president's relationships with state, local, and tribal governments. I also had a policy role leading the immigration team, in which I collaborated with the Domestic Policy Council (DPC) team, led by Melody Barnes. At the end of 2011, Melody announced that she was leaving the White House. I knew right away that the DPC job was a much better fit for me than the job I was doing. Intergovernmental affairs is all about building relationships, and I was itching to get back to a full-time policy role. I went to Valerie to seek her advice on putting my hat in the ring for the DPC job. She smiled and said, "Oh, I already threw it in the ring for you."

It was encouraging to have a vote of confidence from a boss who believed in me, but Bill Daley was the chief of staff. He would have a substantial role in the decision, and he didn't have a feel for me or my work. I learned later, after he left the White House, that Bill had spoken to a couple of journalists who were writing books about President Obama's first term, and he conveyed to them that he was angry that I had been promoted to the domestic policy job. In those books, I come across as a second-tier staffer, much less qualified for a senior job than the people Bill preferred. In one account, my promotion was the last straw that led to Bill's departure from the White House. In another, this incident is in a section describing the president's efforts to appeal to Latinx voters, which gives the impression that I owed my job to my ethnicity more than my ability.

The experience of going forward for that promotion and learning later of Bill's reaction had the strange effect of bolstering my confidence and shattering it at the same time. Getting the job of course bolstered my confidence. The shattering isn't hard to understand, though. For starters, I already felt the doubts that lots of people, especially women, tend to feel when we are in high-level roles that traditionally have been held by white men. We know some people have trouble picturing us in those roles—sometimes we have trouble picturing ourselves in them, too—and it's not unusual to wonder, sitting in a room full of high-powered people, Do I really belong here? Do they see me as someone who belongs at this table? The White House is about as high-powered as it gets. I don't think I was the only one with some degree of imposter syndrome.

I did have a few years at the White House under my belt by then, and I had the confidence that comes from doing your job well in a way that has earned you the respect of at least those of your colleagues who have seen your work. Valerie Jarrett was the kind of person that I could turn to for feedback, and I knew she wouldn't hold back if there was something I needed to do to up my game. I could walk into her office and say, "That meeting didn't go well. Please help me sort through what went wrong," and know that it was a safe space to have a conversation that would make a difference. I knew I could count on her to help sharpen my skills, and I also knew I could count on her to tell me the truth, even when it was hard, which meant I would never have to wonder about how I was doing. In a fast-paced, high-stakes workplace that usually offers zero feedback, this was a rare and wonderful thing.

But a few years at the White House had also taught me what happens to people who are perceived as being not quite up to their jobs. Nobody tells them. Everybody just starts working around them. These people don't get invited to the meetings where decisions are made, or worse, they get invited to the "fake meeting" where a large group of people are consulted and have some input, which is followed by the more secretive "real meeting," where a much smaller group makes the decision. As a result, everyone is constantly monitoring who is meeting with whom and wondering whether their capacity to do their job is slipping because of what they are or aren't included in. When you're working at that velocity, you tend to gather people you need in the room who are at their very sharpest, and you forge forward. Sometimes people get left behind. To say that this can be a breeding ground for self-doubt doesn't even begin to cover it.

When you're the only Latina in the room, which happened a lot, there's a part of you that wonders whether others see you as a fully formed member of the team, one of the people they will gather to get stuff done, or one of the people they have to have in the room, perhaps for the fake meeting before the real stuff gets done. It may be a sign of weakness to admit this, but I'm being honest. And this creeping doubt got confirmed at a very high level. The chief of staff to the president of the United States implied to a journalist that I wasn't qualified for my job. Twice. So, yeah, that contributed to some self-doubt.

The moment that epitomizes my struggle with the voice in my head telling me I didn't belong in a place like the West Wing occurred in the weeks between my interviews for the DPC job in late 2011 and the moment when the president offered it to me in January 2012. I happened to go to my favorite bookstore in DC and there, on the table, next to each other, were books written by two of the candidates for the job whom Bill Daley had recommended—both white men, both friends of mine, both friends of the president, and both with reputations for brilliance. I looked at their books and it felt as if the universe was telling me something by placing them side by side in front of me. The voice in my head got busy: What was I thinking? How can I possibly be hoping for this job knowing that the chief of staff is pushing these two extremely eminent guys? I love them both! So does the president! WHAT WAS I THINKING? The part of me that knew that I could master the job and do it well was there, but it was out-shouted pretty heavily that day.

I wish I could say I let go of the doubt once the president offered me the job, but that wouldn't be true. Of the five years I served as domestic policy director, I spent a good two wondering whether my colleagues on the senior team were taking me seriously and whether what I was experiencing was politeness or respect. I learned in the end that it was the latter, but it took me a while.

Kathy Ko Chin, who leads the Asian & Pacific Islander American Health Forum and serves with me as a trustee of the Kresge Foundation, has had the same kind of experience. When I asked her whether she has ever been asked to be in the room simply because someone decided that they needed some diversity, she answered with an emphatic "yes." Kathy is regularly the only Asian American in a room full of civil rights leaders of all kinds. And because her community is smaller and less visible than the African American and Latinx communities, combined with the myth that Asian and Pacific Islander Americans are a "model minority" that doesn't experience the same challenges as other groups, she is often shunted to the side. "The first few times, it was really demoralizing, that self-doubt," she told me. "It sucks your soul. 'Let's get a speaker because we need diversity,' but don't take them seriously. I had to get over it and recognize that I was in the room, so I should take advantage to advocate and get things done, not get intimidated by it. It still happens, but now I see it for what it is."

Kathy also describes what this kind of "tokenism" looks like in practice: "I have been on stages and panels where we are literally at the end of the row; the moderator can't even see us. Or I will be at tables where they want me there for diversity, but others take up all the oxygen, and it can be a challenge for our voices to be heard. It's a delicate dance; all of us should be lifting up every community's challenges respectfully. As much as I want to be an ally, I need others to be an ally back."

Kara Bobroff, who founded and serves as the principal and executive director of the Native American Community Academy, a New Mexico charter school that serves a diverse group of students, including students from sixty-two Native American tribes, has much the same experience. For the first half of her career, she was almost always the only Native American principal or educator in the room at any level. She describes constantly having to provide input about what Native students need to educators who assume that they have more expertise than she, even though they are not Native American. She describes one incident in which she made her case from a deep base of knowledge. "Initially," she says, "I had people turn around, look at me, and turn back around and keep talking."

When the Doubt Comes from Within

I don't think it's unusual for anyone who walks into the West Wing for their first day of work to be thinking, "Holy cow, how did I get here? What if I'm not up to the challenge? What if people can tell that I'm not up to the challenge?" When I walked into the West Wing that first day, January 21, 2009, the country was in the middle of an economic free fall of historic proportions. We didn't know where the bottom was or whether we were anywhere near it. We weren't sure we were going to be able to generate the bipartisan support that we needed to get us out of it. We know how the story ends now—that President Obama presided over the longest streak of job growth in the nation's history, adding millions of jobs over seventy-five straight months—but taking the reins of government amid an historic economic crisis was terrifying. Anybody with a shred of honesty and self-awareness would have felt fearful under the circumstances.

But there were lots of other currents of doubt pulling at me, too: Did I have the stamina to work sixteen-hour days? Would I make a mistake that would wind up on CNN fifteen seconds later? What if I made a mistake that got me fired? Could I cope with what everybody told me to expect: a cutthroat atmosphere in which even your friends aren't really your friends? Some of those currents of fear had more-personal roots: Could I handle giving up family time in the precious years I had left with my girls at home? Was I there because I had what it takes to do the job, or was I there because I am a Latina? Could it possibly be both?

Jodi Archambault Gillette, a Native American woman who served with me as associate director of the Office of Intergovernmental Affairs and again as a policy lead at the Domestic Policy Council, was not only the most senior Native American in the White House but possibly the first indigenous woman ever to serve at her level. She felt the same kinds of doubts that I did:

When I first got to the White House, I was homesick and I wasn't sure I was the right person for the position. I was away from my kids, learning new systems, meeting new people. The idea I had in my head was that the person who should be there was a DC insider who knew the systems of government, who aspired to be in the government. My strategy was to make people at home proud of me, to serve them in the best way I can, so the best thing that I could do for myself and for them was to just be honest. Be totally honest. My idea was that the government is not going to like that, people are not going to like the truth about what is out there. Powerful people want to be in an echo chamber. They don't want to hear about the schools and the child abuse and the shortcomings where the government has failed. So my idea was that, no matter what it was, I was just going to tell the truth, even if they don't want to hear it. I wanted to be able to go home and hold my head up high.

Jodi and I were both in our jobs because of our expertise and our lived experience. But people like us, the firsts in our roles, often wonder whether we are there for show. I know for a fact that this wasn't true for Jodi, because I was the person who hired her. We needed what she brought to government, and I watched with great pride and respect as she spoke for her community in ways that moved the ball forward, educating her colleagues — including me — as she went. I was less sure about how others saw me.

I was the most senior Latinx person in the White House, and some of my colleagues likely thought I was the kind of person you would want in the room when Hispanics and immigration are being discussed, but weren't certain I offered much value beyond that. How could they? Most of them had never heard of me. Not that these colleagues weren't wonderful to work with; most of them absolutely were. Not that they didn't believe in diversity — after all, we were all working for the first African American president. But many of them were extremely eminent people. The former president of Harvard was in an office across the hall from mine. It's not that I didn't bring qualifications of my own, but I think it says something that, even after a successful career and the public acknowledgment that goes with it, I still worried that my presence checked a box: nobody could criticize the president for not being inclusive because I was in the room. It's not that my colleagues didn't expect me to do my job, but it felt to me as if I still had to work to earn their respect.

Getting Tested

You will get tested over and over throughout your career. Sometimes you'll have no idea that people are watching, and other times you'll be well aware that you're being tested. You will be able to feel your colleagues watching to see whether you'll rise to the challenge. That's how it happened for me as the president was preparing his first State of the Union Address (which we called SOTU, because Washington is a town of alphabet-soup acronyms) a year into his presidency.

I was already aware at that time that colleagues were assessing whether I was going to play the role of the ethnic outsider who is pushing on her particular issues, or that of a team member who sees the bigger picture. The world that I come from and that it was part of my job to represent was eager for the president to embrace immigration reform, even as we did the vital work of shoring up the economy and reforming a health care system with skyrocketing costs. They decided that the SOTU speech would be a definitive test of his seriousness on our issues. I was getting calls from advocates saying things like, "We need him to say the following five things, and if he doesn't, the reaction is going to be harsh." They were expecting a section on immigration. I was wondering whether there would be a sentence.

The pressures inside the White House were intense. This was going to be the president's first SOTU address. The economy was just beginning to recover, but regular Americans couldn't yet feel that recovery in their lives. We had teams working to suggest and develop speech content on issues like jobs, financial reform, economic growth, education and training, health care, security, Afghanistan and Iraq, nuclear weapons, and Al Qaeda. Amid an epic economic crisis, in a time in which we were fighting two wars, what was clear to us inside the building was that SOTU had to be focused and not three hours long. Outside the building? Everybody in the Latinx advocacy world was focused on telling us what the president should say about immigration.

This was one of my first big tests. I had a strong sense of what the president needed to do for a constituency and issue that mattered to him, but there were huge crosswinds within his party and country blowing back against giving that issue priority, both in the speech and beyond.

After much discussion, it turned out there would be only a single sentence devoted to immigration in the windup to the close of the speech—in a section that touched on an array of other important issues that didn't get their own sections of the speech, either. I had to fight for that last sentence to be there at all, and I had to fight over its content. Because when I first saw the near-final draft of the speech, I found only a sentence fragment, which read, in its entirety: " . . . and *we should continue the work of fixing our broken immigration system—to secure our borders and enforce our laws.*"

It was abundantly clear to me that, as important as enforcement is, if that was the only mention the president made of immigration, without any mention of the positive things that we want to do for and with immigrants, he would have hell to pay in the Latinx community.

David Axelrod, a brilliant, affable, and undeniably pro-immigrant senior advisor to the president who was ultimately responsible for his message and for his politics, was the gatekeeper for SOTU. I sent him a carefully worded email that said something like: "I strongly suggest that we temper the immigration enforcement language with something that shows the president's support for a broader reform." Axe sent a sharp reply. (He was very gracious most of the time. But the twenty-four hours before SOTU—the first one, especially—well, they can be a little tense.) "Cecilia, we are not going to address all of the immigration issues in this speech." I fired back: "I think I know how we can do this—I am coming down." And I took a deep breath and marched from my second-floor office into his office, just steps away from the Oval Office, into one of my first big tests.

As David saw it, the president needed him to produce a focused speech that didn't go off into a million little rabbit holes because of pressures from advocates. As I saw it, the president needed one thing from me, which was to make sure that we got the balance on this issue right, so that his intentions would be clear both to the Latinx community, which wanted to legalize undocumented people, and to the rest of the country, which wanted to know that we took border security seriously. Both of our views were right and seemed mutually exclusive. And the test for me was to understand that my job in that moment was to make it possible for David to do his.

This is the crux of the matter. This is what I have faced over and over in my career. It is, I suspect, a moment that many people of color face when they are in environments in which they're surrounded by other folks who may be well-meaning but don't have the same body of knowledge. To get the job done, they need to know what we know. But they don't always want to know it. And it's much harder when they think they know it but don't.

Here's what that dilemma looks like to me: President Obama is counting on me to prevent a mistake and to assist him in planting the seeds that could help him when the right moment came to get an immigration reform done—the moment when Congress and the country could be persuaded to go with him.

In that moment, David Axelrod needs one thing from me: he needs me to go away. Me and everybody else managing a constituency that wants a forty-five-minute discourse on their issue. He doesn't know me well enough yet to know whether I am the Latina in the White House fighting for my piece of the speech, or a Latina member of the team, bringing her expertise to get the larger job done in a way that still leaves room for immigration. In this moment, I am being tested. Am I going to be an advocate who comes at my colleagues relentlessly and wears them down? Or am I going to assume my tiny piece of responsibility for the larger enterprise and show David a way to do what he needs to do that also addresses immigration in a way that doesn't anger a major constituency?

Whether it's because of gender, race, ethnicity, disability, or LGBTQ status—whatever it is, many of us face moments when we are tested, when we have to be true to what we know and also figure out a way to articulate it that can be heard, can make a difference, and won't knock us out of the circle that allows us to have influence. It's a tremendously difficult balance to strike.

It's possible that I could have been more effective if I had chosen to be a relentless advocate and push for the immigration section that my community expected and deserved, but I don't think so. I chose the other course; I assumed responsibility for the larger enterprise and found a way to make it work. I wrote a sentence for David that dealt with the security issues he knew the country wanted to hear, with an additional clause that signified that the president understood that immigration is also about people. It took all of five minutes, and the tension in the room dissipated the moment David had the sentence in front of him, and he got on with the multitude of other challenges that he needed to work through in the speech. Perhaps just as importantly, he now saw me as someone he could work with, who might bring her own perspective into the room, but who was willing to find ways to align that perspective with the vast range of priorities that every White House has to manage. My choice to find a way forward that worked for everyone positioned me to run the race.

Here is what the speech said:

My Administration has a Civil Rights Division that is once again prosecuting civil rights violations and employment discrimination. We finally strengthened our laws to protect against crimes driven by hate. This year, I will work with Congress and our military to finally repeal the law that denies gay Americans the right to serve the country they love because of who they are. It's the right thing to do. We're going to crack down on violations of equal pay laws—so that women get equal pay for an equal day's work.

And we should continue the work of fixing our broken immigration system—to secure our borders and enforce our laws, *and ensure that everyone who plays by the rules can contribute to our economy and enrich our nation.*

Victory? Hardly. I knew when I wrote the sentence that it did the job for the speech, the president, and the country, but I also knew that it wouldn't begin to address everything that the immigration advocacy world or the Spanish language press expected. Here's how the speech was covered in the Spanish language: "Hispanics Unhappy with Obama for Slighting Immigration Reform" (*Al Dia*, Philadelphia). "Obama Avoids Hispanic Immigrants" (*La Raza*, Chicago). "Only a Few Words for Such a Big Issue" (*La Prensa*, Orlando).

But I am convinced that a victory would not, in the end, have served the people putting on the pressure. In other words, what would have happened if I had fought for and won what they wanted—a whole section of the speech? Remember where the country was at that moment: Mortgages underwater. Unemployment at 10 percent. Student debt soaring. People wondering whether the first African American president has what it takes to put us back on track. The fact that he cared about getting immigration reform done was likely not a message that the country would be able to hear in that moment. If there had been an immigration section, we would probably have had a week of listening to pundits wonder why the president would spend so much time in the SOTU on something so out of touch with where the rest of the country was. That might have made the advocates happy, but I don't think it would have advanced immigration reform.

And in the end, my job was not to make advocates happy. It was to advance the issue, and to make sure the president was positioned for success.

Sometimes running the race means making choices about when to push and when to hold back, to focus on finishing the marathon rather than exhausting yourself on a sprint.

Strategies for Dealing with Doubt

I don't think I can name a single woman of color—no matter how successful—who hasn't wrestled with people who doubt her abilities, as well as with her own internal doubts. Patricia Worthy of Howard Law School describes four strategies that she used to address the doubt that inevitably comes from being a first and from having few models for the role you have taken on. They're the same strategies that I use, and as I speak with other women, the similarities in all our approaches are striking.

Strategy #1: Ask for Feedback

Relentlessly. For Patricia, asking for feedback was a strategy for making public presentations when she wasn't 100 percent sure that she was on track. She was very intentionally acknowledging that she could have possibly made a mistake but could correct it.

Kara Bobroff describes coming out of challenging meetings and pushing her team to assess how she did. She'll say things like, "I'm frustrated. Was I heard? Did I say too much? Was I too apologetic in my presentations? Did I not say it loud enough? Did I not express that clearly, or was that okay?"

She says, "I always ask people that after I have put myself out there." And then she chuckles: "A mentor of mine would always say, 'I don't think white guys get out of their meeting and ask themselves, "Was that okay?" They don't hold back when they're thinking about running for office or going after a senior level role. They never ask the question, "Should I do this?" They're like, "I'm going to do this, or I should be the one who gets to do this."""

I tended to quietly ask for feedback from my colleagues, as well. I figured that if I gave them an opportunity to help me see my strengths and weaknesses, some of them would take me up on it and I would up my game. The risk, of course, was showing weakness, but I have learned not to care about that, because strength, in the end, comes from doing your job well. And frankly, I see asking for feedback as a sign of strength.

I asked for feedback and I got it. Some of it was reassuring; I got affirmation that I was doing my job well, and advice on what I could do better. Best of all, I got commiseration from some of the most senior women on the team—seriously talented, brilliant women who seemed confident all the time, but who also struggled with self-doubt. I never would have known had they not told me when I asked for feedback. Some described it as work dysmorphia, much like the body dysmorphia that people with anorexia struggle with: they look in the mirror and what they see doesn't reflect the reality of who they are. We looked in the mirror and saw self-doubt and struggle. But we were capable, talented women giving our best to some of the hardest jobs in the country. My experience of asking for feedback was utterly positive, reassuring, and helpful, and I highly recommend it.

Strategy #2: Do the Work

Kathy Ko Chin calls it being "superbly prepared." Every woman of color whom I spoke with described some version of going miles out of their way to be ultra-prepared. For me, this meant admitting to my staff when I needed to learn things. (Honestly, I was covering all of domestic policy. There is nobody on earth who wouldn't need to learn things.) It also meant scheduling time to get thorough briefings from the policy experts on my team before I attended meetings. I took a fat binder home every weekend to read and study the things I didn't have time to get to during the week. I worked day and night. I dreamed about work. This became such a habit that even now, years after leaving the White House, I still wake up from dreams in which I am wrestling to find the answer to a policy question. I'm still working in my sleep.

Strategy #3: If You Have a Team, Empower Them

Patricia Worthy makes no bones about it: she hired the best people and made sure they were people of color or women, to convey that we can do it better. The secret is hiring a good team and giving them the tools they need to excel. At the White House, instead of expecting my team to transfer all knowledge to me so that I could represent them in meetings, I worked every chance I could to make sure they were the experts in the room.

This may sound obvious, but I found that it took some courage and confidence to lead in a way that demonstrated that the people on my team were the true policy experts and that I was more of an orchestra conductor. You don't have to play each instrument to perfection when you're the conductor; you are getting that perfection out of your players.

I would add to Patricia's wisdom here by encouraging you to form your own personal team even if you don't have one at work. Tyra Mariani wishes that when she was told she wasn't "partner material," she had had some peers with whom she could process that assessment and who likely could have helped her see that it was unfair. When Father Rubey told me the Lord had sent him a dream, I could have benefited from discussions with friends or colleagues who could perhaps have seen better than I could that it might be crazy to take that job. In the end, things turned out well for Tyra and for me. But still, the guidance you might benefit from doesn't always need to be from coworkers, particularly if you have other people in your life who can see clearly and who know who you are.

Strategy #4: Be True to You

Every woman of color whom I spoke with while writing this book found strength in who she is and in the community she comes from and represents. Each of us is aware of our skills and strengths, and we each found ways to bring that awareness into the room as a hedge against doubt.

I know that I don't have the conventionally recognized brilliance of the two guys whom Bill Daley preferred for my job. No question. But I am really good at reading a room and determining what people want and need in order to make a decision. I build strong teams and find ways to make them shine. I run a heck of a meeting, giving everyone a chance to have their say while keeping things running on time. I know some policy issues well, and I know how these policies affect the most vulnerable, the folks most in need of opportunity, which mattered deeply to President Obama. I bring a range of experience into the room that wouldn't otherwise be there because of who I am and what I have done for the past thirty years. By focusing on who I am and what I brought to the job, rather than what I lacked compared to the dazzling people all around me, I built a sense of confidence that served me well in a really hard job. And having learned how to focus on those things, I find I have new reservoirs of fearlessness that I didn't have when I first walked into the White House. Post–White House me has been through the fire, and she is stronger than pre–White House me.

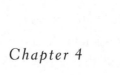

Chapter 4

ON FEAR AND FEARLESSNESS

DOUBT IS THE VOICE INSIDE YOUR HEAD THAT TELLS YOU THAT maybe you don't belong, aren't up to it, or don't have something to offer. I think of fear as something different. Fear is the knowledge that what you're doing is hard and that you might fail. You can be utterly confident and still feel fear. We had a saying at the White House, especially in those first, intense years: "Hard things are hard." And sometimes they're scary.

Fear is real, but it doesn't have to be an obstacle. In fact, I think of it now as a friend. Some of my most vivid memories from my professional journey are of the things that scared me the most—not so much because they were scary, but because I learned so much from them.

It's Not Just You

Here's what I learned in the pressure cooker of the White House. Everybody walks around looking utterly confident. They seem to know a lot that you don't know. They look like they might have the answers to all the hard questions. Except that, for all they know, they're not omniscient. And if you are bold enough to ask them, most will admit that sometimes they're scared to death. Fear is human. Fear is common. Fear is normal.

I felt profoundly fearful at the beginning of my time there. The responsibility was huge, and some of the big things that we dealt with, both expected and unexpected, were objectively just plain frightening. We were in the midst of an epic financial crisis, with the economy shedding hundreds of thousands of jobs a month, and nobody knew where the bottom was. We faced the H1N1 flu pandemic—which turned out to be unusually dangerous to children—while the president's cabinet members were still getting confirmed by the Senate and we were still figuring out where the bathrooms were in the West Wing. A year later, the *Deepwater Horizon* oil rig exploded in the Gulf of Mexico, causing an oil spill at the bottom of the ocean that went on for months. In our lighter moments, we would joke that we saw everything but a plague of locusts.

I was on the team that approved disaster requests from governors after ice storms, hurricanes, tornadoes, and earthquakes. I had no idea how many deadly storms happen every year in America—*so many deadly storms*—until I had to see them up close. I remember getting a call from Governor Steve Beshear of Kentucky when I had been on the job only a few days. In his charming southern drawl, he said something like, "Thanks so much for taking my call. We have had a terrible ice storm here, and I have nursing homes that need generators. I'm about to do a press conference, and I'm going to tell the press that I have spoken to the White House about a disaster declaration because I'm talking to you." At the time, I didn't yet know how the disaster declaration process worked, and thanks to the governor's shrewd call, I realized that if anything happened to any of those people in those nursing homes, we were going to be responsible. I sat at my desk thinking, "This could be the first crisis of the Obama adminis-tration, and at the moment, I'm the only person in the building who even knows that it's happening." At that moment, I had a lot to learn about disaster declarations, but about six hours later, the governor had what he needed, and I really needed a glass of wine.

In every one of those situations it was hard not to have that voice in my head asking, "So what happens if you get this wrong?" During the H1N1 pandemic, a team of us were briefed in the situation room by members of the national security team calmly showing us charts of the number of people who fell sick and died in the flu pandemic of 1919 after being exposed during a single parade in St. Louis. This presentation was followed by a deeply terrifying analysis of what might happen if the virus mutated and we were unable to come up with a vaccine quickly. Sitting at that table with some of the country's best and brightest, I could see that, whatever their inspiring qualities and no matter how bril-liant they were, they had their foibles, too. We had debates and even arguments. There was no clear, right answer, no wisdom that descended on the room from on high; just hard decisions, debated vigorously, which landed on the president's desk for him to make the hard choices. What if we failed? Fear seems appro-priate for that kind of situation.

Because I was aware of fear as my constant companion, I did a bold thing: I asked some of the others who were there whether they felt it, too. You bet they did. Sometimes the men were more reluctant to admit it than the women, but I learned that fear wasn't exclusive to me; it was true for all of us. I found that strangely comforting. And I had the most respect for the people who were willing to admit it. It's not just that they didn't see it as a sign of weakness; they recognized fear and didn't let it stop them. That's what courage is.

Feeling fear at the White House wasn't just about life or death situations. Everything you did—every email, meeting, and public event—brought the possibility of scrutiny. Sometimes even scandal. Deesha Dyer felt this fear profoundly. She started at the White House as an intern, moved on to other jobs, and ultimately became First Lady Michelle Obama's social secretary, which is a senior-level position with huge responsibilities that include overseeing every major White House social event. She told me she was scared every day.

"I was like, oh my God, let me not mess up this dinner. Let me not mess up the pope's visit," she told me. "Because for me, the stakes are so high. It's not reversible. This is a job where you can't put out a correction statement." But Deesha realized there wasn't room for both the doubt that she couldn't do the job and the fear of something going wrong. So, she says, "I focused my fear on being prepared in case something terrible happened on my watch, like a person passing out at a reception with 800 people. That was always my fear because I knew there was no do-over. It's not like the pope is going to come again."

Jodi Archambault Gillette knew fear, too. She remembers one terrifying moment when she felt she had to say something difficult to President Obama himself. He had just traveled to North Dakota with the first lady to visit the Standing Rock Sioux Tribe, of which Jodi is a member. He was so moved by the visit, particularly by the young people who shared their deep personal hardships with him, that he called a meeting of staff and cabinet to develop ideas for how to respond. He had tears in his eyes for the first half of the meeting. In the spirit of brainstorming with the team, he made a suggestion that Jodi knew would not be welcome in her community. "I had to tell him that this idea wouldn't work, that it's not what the people of Standing Rock would have asked for," Jodi says. "I had to say that in front of all those people. He said, 'Fair enough,' and dropped the idea. Even though I started the sentence 'with all due respect,' I wasn't sure that I should have said that."

I was Jodi's boss at the time, and she looked very calm to me as she told the president what he needed to hear. I didn't know until I asked her later that she had found the experience terrifying. I frequently had to remind my team—and myself—that correcting the president of the United States was our job. He expected that of us; if we failed to do that, we were undermining his ability to do the best possible job. But that doesn't mean that it didn't take a little courage to do it in the moment.

As I got more used to working at the White House and dealing with what felt like the constant awareness of being terrified, I finally came to a major realization about fear with the help of my friend Robert Gass, a leadership coach who generously spent time with me during my White House years. I remember telling him, "I think I'm just not doing a good job conquering this fear thing. I feel it every day." His wisdom: "You know why you're feeling fear? Because your job is scary." He finally convinced me that conquering fear was the wrong goal. Fear is normal. I was paying attention, so I could see it, feel it, and name it. Scary things are scary, in any workplace, family, or life. The issue isn't getting rid of fear. The right question is, "What are you going to do with it?"

Fear Can Be Motivating, So Use It Well

The first lesson that I learned from fear, which has become a reflex for me, is to increase my confidence by making sure I am as well prepared as possible for whatever I'm facing.

Anyone who has worked closely with me will likely admit—maybe even with an eye roll or two—that I am not ashamed to ask for help when I am preparing something, and I am willing to go to great lengths to do it.

The first time I testified before Congress, I was still in my twenties. Worse, I was testifying against a bill introduced by two titans of the Senate: Alan Simpson, a famously colorful Republican senator from Wyoming; and Ted Kennedy, a legendary Democrat from Massachusetts. My job was to explain to them that their bill would have a devastating consequence on family-sponsored immigration that they might not have anticipated. I knew going in that the best I could hope for was that they would agree to consider some alternatives. More likely, they would find what I had to say frustrating, insulting, or embarrassing.

Moreover, the point person on Senator Kennedy's staff, Michael Myers (who later became a friend, not to mention a legendary leader of the senator's staff), was not excited that I was the person whom my organization sent to testify. I vividly remember calling to tell him that my boss, Raul Yzaguirre, was not available and was sending me in his stead. "Please ask your boss to reconsider that," he said in his quiet way, no doubt worried that we were sending a kid in place of the CEO at a critical moment in the formation of key legislation. I dutifully reported to Raul that Senator Kennedy's staff had sent a clear signal that they wanted him and not me. Raul looked at his calendar, determined that he couldn't make the timing work, and said, "So rise to the occasion."

I dropped everything and focused on preparing for that hearing. I studied and asked colleagues to talk me through some of the finer points of analysis that I needed to understand and be able to explain. I asked still more colleagues to do a mock hearing to pepper me with the toughest questions they could think of and to challenge me when I couldn't explain things well. One of them, my friend Lisa Navarrete, did such a fierce impression of Senator Simpson that when I was in front of the real senator, he seemed easygoing by comparison.

This was at a moment when I was a woman in my mid-twenties, trying to break into a field dominated by older and more experienced men. I was aware of not wanting to look stupid or weak in front of them, but my most important fear was that I would fail in my job for that hearing, which was to successfully highlight why that bill would have been harmful to the people my organization served. And that fear—the one that had to do with purpose—allowed me to overcome more personal fears: that my colleagues would judge me for not knowing everything and that they would see me as weak for asking questions and making mistakes as I practiced. The key is this: I may have had a pit of fear in my stomach getting ready for that hearing, but by focusing on the big picture I overcame my fear of asking for help, of asking questions that revealed that I still had things to learn, and of showing my vulnerability to colleagues at a moment when I still needed to prove myself.

In the end, with their help, I got the job done. Not only did the hearing go well but I became part of a team that succeeded in making radical changes to that bill and defeating both of those legendary senators in votes on the Senate floor with amendments that improved the outcome. Letting my coworkers in on my preparations didn't undercut my standing with them; if anything, it demonstrated that I was a person willing to work hard and engage many partners in the effort. I may have been the one in the hot seat, but we were all in it together. My accomplishment was also theirs.

As I matured in my career, I remained unafraid to ask questions, to be honest especially when I don't know things, and to enlist the people around me in helping me get ready for challenging or important moments. I would say things like, "I'm going to attempt to explain this point, and I want you to critique when I'm not clear or when I'm getting it wrong." When I first got to the White House, I confess that I did wonder whether I would diminish my stature by asking a lot of questions as I prepared for meetings and presentations. But I kept my focus on the importance of delivering the goods when I was in the room for the key decision, not on my own stature.

It's entirely possible that some of my colleagues felt that this behavior—especially admitting to staff that I still had things to learn—proved me to be a lightweight. And I did have some moments of worry that if they thought the one Latina in the room was a lightweight, they would think all Latinas were not ready for prime time. Was I tanking our one shot at succeeding in this kind of job?

Here's the lesson I learned: It doesn't matter what they think. It's not worth spending an ounce of energy worrying about it. There was not a single person in the West Wing, of any race or gender, from the president on down, who didn't have things to learn. The result of your effort is much more important, and that will ultimately speak louder than anything else. In the end, nobody who mattered held it against me when I owned that, although I knew a lot, I didn't know everything. My team and my peers seemed to appreciate that I was working as hard as I could to honor their expertise and get to the best result. And the way we worked together underscored what we all understood to be true. As a team, we were working to succeed. Any success didn't belong just to me but to us.

There's a second lesson in that: doing the hard work of being ultra-prepared for a scary situation has the corollary benefit of creating an opportunity for leadership. That may sound strange, because we have been taught to think about leadership as giving commands or making big decisions. But leadership can also look like this: I am in a role that will put me out in front, I will have to speak for us all, and I need to know some of what you know to do this well. So, this goal isn't my goal, it's our goal. We will work on it together. I will do my best to honor your expertise by articulating it well at the decision-making moment. Any success is our success. That's how you build successful teams. And the pathway just might start with acknowledging a little bit of fear.

Fear May Be Normal,
but It Doesn't Have to Be In Charge

I learned other important lessons about fear. It may be normal, and it may be a good catalyst to make sure you're prepared for tough moments, but it's also all in our heads. Or in my case, in my stomach. That's where I feel it most.

I have learned over time that fear doesn't deserve the power that I sometimes give it. Here's an illustration of what I mean: sometimes the people we work with have personalities or styles that generate fear. These are people who may regularly wield their power to fire you, embarrass you in front of your peers, or make it difficult for you to do what you need to do. That can certainly have a motivating effect, but it can also keep people on edge, thinking about protecting their own interests rather than doing their jobs, and spending altogether too much energy avoiding uncomfortable situations.

The first chief of staff to serve President Obama, Rahm Emanuel, has a famously foul-mouthed and abrasive leadership style. He is a lifelong public servant with a great heart who presided over a period of enormous legislative accomplishment as President Obama's chief of staff, and I have a lot of respect and affection for him. But Rahm's style generates fear and discomfort for his coworkers, and he's not above leveraging those things to get what he wants out of his team.

He convened an occasionally terrifying morning meeting for the senior staff every day, in which everyone was pretty much required to report something brief for the benefit of the rest of the group. If you had nothing to report a couple of days in a row, you'd get a dressing down. And if he believed that you were guilty of some transgression, he wasn't above yelling at you in front of the thirty or so people sitting in the Roosevelt Room of the West

Wing, which is where we met every day at 8:30 a.m., about three paces from the Oval Office. Most of the senior staff had a turn in the hot seat, and I was no exception. I think we all prepared somewhat anxiously for that meeting, hoping that our turn to be yelled at wouldn't come that day. The feeling many of us had preparing for that meeting? Fear. No question.

I knew right away the day it was my turn to get yelled at. I had spoken to a reporter from the *New York Times* the previous day. I had cleared the interview with the communications team, who had assigned someone to sit with me and listen in. I repeated on the record something that the president had said himself many times, which is that he intended to tackle immigration reform. For some reason, the reporter sounded surprised, as if I were saying something new. It was clear to me that he was going to report my words as part of a significant story, so I went down to Rahm's office to give his team a heads-up that the *Times* was going to run a story framing immigration reform as a "new" priority.

When the story ran the next morning, I was horrified: it was on the front page and portrayed the president's often-stated desire to reform the immigration system as a shocking new development. On the surface, that's not much of a problem, but it came at a time when we were trying to focus press coverage on the work the president was doing to create jobs and move the economy out of its crisis. Any headline on another subject was one less headline on our message. And Rahm was furious.

At 8:30, as I slid into my seat next to my boss, Valerie Jarrett, knowing that she had been in the 7:30 meeting with Rahm and a smaller group of senior advisors, I whispered to her, "How much trouble am I in?" "So much trouble," she whispered back. So, I braced myself for what was coming. And it came: the string of invectives, the cursing, the "how dare you decide what our message is going to be today?"

I felt strangely calm. I hadn't committed the great sin that I was being accused of, which is to go around the communications team to advance my own issue. I had worked with them on what seemed like a small story, and the newspaper had gotten the emphasis wrong. I waited for the storm to pass. Rahm was interested in making a point to the group, not in having a discussion with me about what had happened, so I didn't respond to his yelling. And when the storm was over, I felt kind of liberated. The worst thing I had feared had happened. My colleagues had all seen Rahm do this before. There weren't real consequences to the yelling other than some moments of extreme discomfort. I hadn't gotten fired, and by the time the meeting was over, everybody was off to do their fourteen hours of intense work for the day, including me. The total effect of experiencing the worst thing that could happen in that morning meeting was about three minutes of ugliness while being yelled at, but no actual harm. I was never afraid of that meeting after that, nor was I afraid of anybody's temper.

More importantly, I learned a key lesson about how to manage fear in situations that are legitimately scary. Play out your fear. What's the worst thing that could happen? Getting yelled at? Getting fired? Having my firing be the thing they talk about on cable news all day? I have seen people go through all those things. It's oddly empowering to picture the very worst that could happen: Yep. Getting fired would feel terrible. What would I do? I'd walk out of the building. I'd go home to my wonderful family. I would endure some humiliation and then get on with my life. I would eventually find another job. People survive that. I could survive it. I find that once I walk through it in my head, the fear loses its fangs.

That experience helped me focus on having the right motivation for preparing for a scary situation. Think about it: in the situation I was in, is the proper focus to do all that you can to avoid the yelling, or to focus on doing your job well? The difference between the former and the latter can be considerable. What I learned from getting screamed at in the Roosevelt Room has turned out to be powerful and positive: If I make a mistake, I will own it and do everything I can to make it right. And if there's yelling, I will totally survive it. That lesson has come in handy more than once.

Deesha Dyer had an even more deliberate and effective strategy for putting her fear into perspective. When she was working at the White House, she also volunteered once a week at different organizations serving people who were grappling with difficult things, including at a homeless shelter and a place where women lived while they were restarting their lives outside of prison walls. Deesha didn't feel safe sharing her fears at the office, so she shared them with the women whom she got to know while volunteering. Some women shared with her about the fear they'd felt going to prison and gave her great advice: they told her that they were scared, "but you have to just breathe. I told myself every day the sun's going to rise and the sun's going to set and the pope's going to come or whatever's going to happen whether I'm ready or not. So it wasn't like we could stop this train for me to get ready. It was never that. It was always: you just have to get through it."

Sometimes the way to handle fear is to remember that you're not alone in feeling it. And if other people grappling with difficult things can survive their challenges, you can survive yours.

When You Have to Say a Difficult Thing

One typical source of fear—or at least discomfort—is the situation in which you are the only person in the room who sees something that others don't see. It might be something about people like you—especially if you're an only in the room—or it might be something else. Your companions all believe they understand something, or they are concocting a plan that's missing something major, and you're the skunk at the party who points out the thing that they don't know, didn't consider, or don't agree with—something that might make them uncomfortable. In my experience, this happens to women all the time, especially to women of color.

For example, I have been following a vibrant conversation among journalists who are women of color, who find that they are constantly in this situation. Issues of race and gender are in the news, the subject of national debate. They might be the only women of color in the newsroom with direct experience of the issues that are getting reported on. They get attacked as "biased" if they raise what they know by virtue of just being who they are, but if they don't speak up, their colleagues often miss important angles to the stories that they're reporting, or worse, get the stories totally wrong.

In an article for *Nieman Lab*, Tanzina Vega, a journalist whom I greatly admire who is also a professor of journalism at Princeton University, writes, "[O]ne of the biggest mistakes the media punditry made about the 2016 election was underestimating the power of racist rhetoric in the campaign. There was a disconnect between what journalists of color were seeing and what white reporters were seeing, what white audiences were consuming versus what black and brown audiences were reading." She goes on to make the point that newsrooms, which are still overwhelmingly white and male, play a role in creating many of the harmful racial narratives that the rest of us live with.

You may find yourself in some variant of that situation: you have information that is important to a discussion or a decision at work, but what you have to say might make others uncomfortable. Or you might feel that you need to say something because your coworkers are taking the conversation in a direction that is so misguided that it makes you uncomfortable. You might be feeling that you need to speak just to be true to yourself. It's not easy.

I had my own variant on this situation the day I met then senator Obama, when he was newly elected to the Senate and learning the ropes in Washington. He invited some progressive and civil rights leaders to a dinner at the George Hotel, and my boss, NCLR president Janet Murguía, couldn't go, so she sent me in her place. I remember that the group consisted of a lot of white and African American men, because that's who was running the major progressive and civil rights groups at the time. There must have been other women there, though I don't remember who. I know for sure that I was the only Latinx person in the room.

The others spent a lot of time talking about some of the wonky battles of the moment: a push to extend unemployment insurance, to protect Social Security from being privatized by the Bush administration, and to protect Senate Democrats' ability to filibuster potential Bush nominees to the Supreme Court. As they talked, I sat there thinking, "yes, this is all important, but I'm here to speak for the Latinx community, and this is not at all what we are focused on. In fact, some of this doesn't affect us very directly at all." I sat there with my heart pounding a little, knowing that I was going to have to be the skunk at the party, which is a familiar role, because I am frequently the only woman or the only Hispanic person in rooms all over Washington.

When there was an opening in the conversation, I politely spoke up. "Senator, these are all important issues, but if you're interested in getting to know the Hispanic community, I have to say that there are other issues that people are more focused on," I said. I went on to explain that 40 percent of us weren't covered by unemployment insurance in the first place, so extending it wouldn't help us much. The other issues would affect us, but they were not nearly as top of mind as jobs, health care, and education. The rest of the group was polite and quiet for a moment, but I could practically hear them thinking, "Well, that was kind of awkward and off message," and then the conversation went right back to where it was before I spoke. *Okay*, I thought. *I have said what I have to say. Let me step quietly out of here at the first opportunity.* When the dinner broke up and I made my way to the door, I found my way blocked by Senator Obama's advisor, Michael Strautmanis, who is so tall that he had to lean way over to say in his gentle voice, "The Senator was very interested in what you had to say. He'd like to hear more."

That meeting was my first conversation with Obama, the first of many briefings and conversations that led to him asking me to serve in the White House. And it was one of many "skunk at the party" moments throughout my career. To be true to myself and my role, I had to say something that stopped the conversation cold, that seemed off message to everybody else in the room.

They aren't particularly comfortable, those moments. They are even more uncomfortable when you're an only—the only woman in the room, the only person of color, the only person with your range of experience. But I find that two things make them less uncomfortable. The first is knowing your stuff and taking strength from that knowledge. I find it much easier to say things that others might not be ready to hear when I have a firm grasp of the facts and can explain them clearly and concisely. I had facts at my disposal, and I had a range of experience that was unique in that room. People may not be happy with what you're adding to the conversation, but you're the only person who can provide that perspective, and they need your input whether they know it or not. The more you convey that you know what you're talking about, the more confidence you will have and the more convincing you will be.

The second thing that makes these moments less uncomfortable is knowing what's important. It helps enormously to have a deep understanding of your purpose, the thing that you are in the room—or even on the planet—to achieve. In that room with Senator Obama, I brought decades of knowledge and experience not only as a policy expert, but as the one Latina on the premises. I knew that I was in the room to speak from that experience, for the people I have spent a lifetime serving, and as long as I stayed true to that purpose, I would be okay. When I got to the White House, I could be sure that the president knew exactly who I was when he asked me to serve, and I was confident that what he wanted from me was to bring my expertise and perspective into the room even—and especially—when I was the only one who brought it. Knowing your stuff and knowing what's important doesn't always make the conversation easier, but it absolutely gives you the foundation and the confidence to say what you need to say with authority and conviction.

Knowing what's important is how Pramila Jayapal conquered a crippling fear of public speaking. You wouldn't know it to look at her, giving eloquent speeches on the floor of the House of Representatives or in front of television cameras with the US Capitol behind her, but she was not always a confident public speaker. Indeed, she was an utterly terrified public speaker. When Pramila was a young professional working in the public health field, she would call in sick to avoid having to give a presentation. If she was in a meeting and needed to ask a question, she would freeze, lose track of what everyone else was saying, and then not be able to get the question out. It is impossible for me to reconcile the eloquent congresswoman whom I know with that frightened young professional, so I asked her how she got past it.

Pramila began an unexpected career as an advocate after the terrorist attacks of 9/11, when a lot of South Asian, Arab, and Muslim Americans started to face hate crimes, harassment, and discrimination from people who couldn't see them as the patriotic Americans who they are. This so angered Pramila, who is South Asian herself, that she started to stand up and speak out about what she was seeing in her community. She told me, "I remember being with all of these Somali women who had their grocery stores shut down by the FBI and there was no time to be scared because this was serious. And it just never occurred to me to be afraid."

At one point, Pramila wrote a book, and went on a book tour. She told me, "At my very first book reading I almost threw up before going out because there were 300 people there. All of my friends came, and I thought, 'I can't go out there.' I was literally holding my stomach, and then I finally just sort of took a few deep breaths and I went out and I realized I was just reading from what I had spent two years working on. I felt more and more confident, and when I finished, there were questions. I realized that I like answering questions about something I know and care about." Pramila had a strong sense of purpose and an enormous body of knowledge and experience. That's what mattered to her—and it mattered so much that it overwhelmed her fear of speaking in public.

If You're in the Room, Bring Your Whole Self

When I talk about the things that I have found difficult or scary, I refer a lot to whether I think my actions cost me my standing in the eyes of others. Caring about what others think about me is sometimes a real concern, and I don't think that's true only for me. It's pretty human to measure yourself against what you can pick up about others' perceptions of you. Sometimes we get direct feedback, but more often we are reading the signs about how people respond to us, and perhaps making adjustments based on what we think we see.

I have come to believe that this is particularly true for people of color, especially in situations in which we are a minority or perhaps the only one in the room. I have certainly felt it, even in rooms that were entirely friendly. For eight years I was with people who were working for the first African American president. They were believers in diversity; they were inclined to welcome my view before I ever walked into the room. But over thirty years in Washington, I have never lost the sense that I wasn't quite in the club. For eight years, I traveled in circles that Washington elites travel in, and I've been the recipient of envelopes addressed to The Honorable Cecilia Muñoz inviting me to black-tie dinners with celebrities in attendance. Throughout, I have felt something like an anthropologist observing the habits of an exotic species. I have never felt quite like an insider, even when I worked in an insider's job.

Now, this could be owing entirely to the fact that I am a policy nerd, an introvert, and not exactly a social butterfly. But honestly, this feeling doesn't just apply to Washington social circles. I felt it in the Obama White House as well, not because my colleagues weren't lovely to work with; they mostly were. But even in a place that honored diversity and lived it, I could see that some of what I brought into the room was outside of what my colleagues were familiar with, outside of their knowledge base and sometimes even their comfort zone. That's part of what diversity is for: to challenge people and to provide more perspectives to get to a better result. But this puts a lot of responsibility on those of us who are the others at the table. Our job is to speak, explain, bring our experience and expertise into the conversation, and make ourselves heard and understood. It's not always easy, even when you're in a room full of people already inclined to be open to hearing you. And it can be tough when you're not.

In a way, the experiences that seem the toughest are the ones that bother me the least, like getting yelled at on television by people who are not interested in learning what I have to offer. Their goal is to make their point by giving me a verbal lashing, and I stay focused on my own goal, which is to make a point. I have done plenty of that, and while I don't think of this as a particularly fun experience, I tend not to get worked up about it. It's worth dissecting what is scary about this kind of situation as opposed to what's in your imagination. The yelling can't hurt you. Your primary concern is to avoid losing your cool and make sure you make a coherent argument. Your job in that kind of situation is to make your point of view available to anybody who may be watching who is prepared to listen, and to deny the shouters the opportunity to mischaracterize your community or your position, because you are there to describe it yourself. As long as I'm prepared, I find it easy to stay focused in that kind of situation.

Strangely, I find it much harder to be the person at a friendly table explaining something about my own experience that others don't know and may not have considered. For some reason, it's much tougher for me to explain what I know when I am among people who believe themselves to be well informed but who don't know what I know. It can feel easier to just let it go and not explain the thing that they don't see, because it's easier to get along that way and to feel more like one of them. Sometimes the thing that I know they're missing doesn't really matter. Sometimes it does. But what if I get it wrong? What if I become the pest who is always popping up to explain things that aren't relevant?

I remember how mightily I struggled to explain to a very friendly member of the editorial board of the *Washington Post* why I was so offended when the Clinton administration invited me to a meeting with hundreds of other advocates, and I was the only attendee asked by the security screeners whether I was a US citizen, because of my name and ethnicity. I had drafted an opinion editorial making the point that this kind of discrimination is harmful, and the editor, who was inclined to be sympathetic, didn't understand the harm because the situation was so far outside of his experience. The way he saw it, once I had overcome the obstacle to getting into the room, there was no harm done.

To me, it was so obviously harmful to set up an obstacle that applied only to the one Latina in the room that I struggled to find the words to explain it. Perhaps when you face unnecessary obstacles over and over because of who you are, it's easy to see the injustice. But it's not easy to explain to someone who hasn't had the experience. It took me several attempts to explain it to him on the phone and several tries to convey it clearly in writing. I could feel my friend getting annoyed at my persistence. I started to wonder whether I was jeopardizing my relationship with an important contact at the *Post*. I almost gave up. But I concluded that it was worth keeping at it. I believe that if you're going to be at the table, it's important to be fully there, as yourself, with all that you know and have experienced. Having worked so hard to get there, I want to bring my whole self, and there are parts of my Latina self that others might not instinctively understand.

Kara Bobroff is in this situation all the time, frequently the only indigenous person in the room. "When I was younger, I experienced a lot of internalized racism . . . and really tried to fit in," she told me. "I also felt a sense of shame and didn't actually consciously know why. As I started to understand who I was in college and in life, and then started to get a stronger grounding in my early twenties, I became aware that I was seen as a bridge builder. I don't think that was an intentional strategy that I set out to execute on, but it was something that people said that I had the ability to do: to work across difference. I think that comes from my experience relating both in a white world or a white population and across economic status, as well as being part of a community that did not historically have access." Now that she is older and has a lot more experience and personal growth under her belt, Kara feels less need to fit in and more compelled to speak up: "We don't have a lot of time in our lives to really impact what it is we're trying to change. So now I'm at a point in my life where I want to push forward, do what we can as much as we can, as fast as we can. So I will definitely draw upon those experiences I've had across difference, and also strongly encourage our peers who I know could do more as well and not hold back. I'm comfortable doing that and I'm also ready to do that because it's needed, and the work is urgent."

To me, bringing my whole self into the situations that I'm in means being authentic. It means having the presence of mind to understand what might be different about my experience, and what about that difference might be worth bringing into the room for others to consider. Being aware of the difference is a constant, daily thing, but identifying what might be worth saying out loud is trickier, more nuanced. If I'm paying attention, I have learned that when something is pulling at me and my heart is starting to beat faster because I have a sense that there's something that I really need to say—something that might be hard to say—usually, that pull means that it's something important. The fear is actually telling me something; it's conveying urgency.

Kara must deal with people who don't expect her to bring expertise into the room. Some don't even expect her to speak English. She has learned to use data to demonstrate that her methods and the school she leads are making a difference. We have all kinds of other sources of data that help us make the case, both about what goes wrong in America, as well as what can go right. There are videos of police violence. There is new data on economic disparities by race, discrimination in access to housing, and differential treatment in the health care system based on biases that are so deeply ingrained that some of us don't even know that they are there. There is also data to show that leaders like Kara are making a difference, that progress is possible. All of this can help us see what we haven't been seeing, and maybe even shock the conscience of anyone who is paying attention. One question that I ask myself, when my heart is pounding with a point that feels like it needs to be made, is whether I have the data to back it up and whether I am prepared to make the point in a way that people can hear.

But as important as data is, our most important tool remains our voices, our capacity to tell stories about what we experience and why others should care. I think that this is at the heart of my discomfort when I am in situations in which I know something so deeply from experience that I can't always find the words to make it known to others who have never gone through the same thing. It's important to me to get it right, so I practice.

If you ever have the misfortune to pull up next to me while I am at a stoplight in my car, you may see me engaged in a lively conversation with myself. Chances are I am refining an argument, practicing my lines in the hope of becoming more effective, more persuasive. Maybe I'm working out some anger so that I don't express that anger during the conversation. Not that anger isn't appropriate, but I have found that it's only rarely an effective tool for persuasion, and for me, the most important thing is whether I can impact the people I am with. If I can't help them see what they don't see, I will keep at it, because I believe that's how we move forward.

There are countless sources of inspiration to draw from, epic moments in which people have used their voices, stories, and experience to teach us all something that we didn't know about how others are treated, those moments that help us see injustices that have been hidden to us. The African Americans who fought for civil rights in the 1950s and '60s used their bodies to show the rest of America the terrible lengths that segregationists and white supremacists went to in order to deny them voting rights and other civil rights. The late Cesar Chavez put his body on the line, fasting to draw attention to the conditions in which farmworkers live and work in the United States. Anita Cameron, an African American disability rights activist, has been arrested more than 130 times as she engages in nonviolent protest in support of disability and LGBTQ rights. One of those protests was a "die-in" on Capitol Hill against the repeal of the Affordable Care Act. The die-in became famous because of shocking photos of the way police removed protesters from their wheelchairs, dragging them out of the room. Anita gave a powerful statement to the online publication *Quartz* that people shocked by the photos should "concentrate on why we're there and not how we're being treated . . . [P]eople look at the disability and they think we are helpless or fragile . . . and that's so far from the truth."

Not every truth-telling moment is as dramatic as Anita Cameron and Cesar Chavez putting their bodies on the line. Tyra Mariani describes a moment when she confronted a group of friends, colleagues, and allies whom she had worked with over many years in the education field:

> I was in a cohort of education leaders. It was a moment when "woke" and "stay woke" were fairly new in the lexicon. We were talking about what was happening in the world, that maybe this was a time to stand up and maybe go to jail over our issues. And just before we were going to take a break in the discussion I remember saying, "I want to talk about how I'm irritated that y'all are now woke." They looked at me and I said, "We have told you about police misconduct. We have told you about young boys and men of color and how the world treats them. And now you seem to get it. You have been in this work for decades. It's like you didn't believe us, because now it seems like you get it. That pisses me off. It says that our voices haven't been enough."
>
> It broke the egg. People had to look in the mirror and say, "I don't know why I didn't get it." We didn't solve the tension,

but we peeled the onion a little bit more. They had to ask themselves, "Why did it take until now for me to get this thing that people of color have been talking about?"

Pramila Jayapal has shown the courage to be authentic in a very public setting, telling us truths that may be hard to say and challenging to hear, but that may also help move us forward. In a committee hearing on a civil rights bill in the House of Representatives, she talked about what she learned from her child: "I didn't intend to say this today, but my beautiful now twenty-two-year-old child told me last year that they were gender nonconforming, and over the last year, I have come to understand from a deeply personal mother's perspective . . . their newfound freedom . . . to rid themselves of some conformist stereotype of who they are, to be able to express who they are at their real core." Later the same year, Pramila wrote an article for the *New York Times* telling the painful story of her abortion in order to help dispel misconceptions about the choices that women make in circumstances like hers.

Our stories are powerful. They can change hearts and minds if we have the courage to tell them. Tyra's and Pramila's experiences show that progress can be much too slow and sometimes requires the courage to confront people in a challenging way. But they also show that the people around you—your neighbors, your coworkers—may not know that they will benefit from understanding your experience, but they will. In fact, the essence of democracy is that we are all in this together. The more we know about and understand one another, the greater our capacity to become the just society that we have aspired to be since our nation's founding. That's how essential our stories and experience truly are.

Chapter 5

FINDING HEROES

LIKE EVERY OTHER PUBLIC SCHOOL STUDENT OF MY ERA, I was fed a steady diet of heroes when I was growing up, people who played important roles in shaping our history and who are lifted on big public occasions. These are all people who offered something important to the world, and they are all pretty conventional heroes. Presidents like Washington, Jefferson, and Lincoln; scientists who produced major breakthroughs, like Isaac Newton, Marie Curie, and Linus Pauling; social and political reformers like Mahatma Gandhi and Susan B. Anthony; great artists and musicians who shaped culture and created things of beauty, like Michelangelo, Beethoven, and George Gershwin—all were big in my family as I was growing up, particularly beloved by my father.

I didn't really think about the people who were presented as heroes, and I certainly didn't go out of my way to learn much about them. Well, I did learn about Beethoven, but only because there was kind of no choice if you were in a household with my dad. We had a formal dinner to celebrate Beethoven's 200th birthday, and my dad subscribed to a mail-order edition of

Beethoven's entire collected works, which arrived in five-record boxes every month for almost two years. But aside from that, they were mostly people you wrote book reports about who didn't seem to have much of a relationship to real life.

You will notice that this steady diet of notables was mostly male, mostly not contemporary, almost entirely of European origin, and not at all Hispanic. When I was younger, I don't think I thought about looking for heroes or role models to help me chart my course in life—aside from the women in my family—because I had little sense that they were out there. I'm not sure that I could name examples of women in public service or in any other public form of leadership until I got to college. The year I graduated, Geraldine Ferraro ran as the vice-presidential candidate on the Democratic ticket with Walter Mondale, and I was mesmerized by her acceptance speech because I had never seen anything like it.

I didn't start thinking about or looking for heroes until much later, and the reason for my search was a rough patch of loss and fear that hit me hard around my fortieth birthday. The first blow came when I was thirty-nine, when a dear friend, Josh Rosenthal, was killed in the 9/11 terrorist attacks on the World Trade Center. I had thought of Josh as my third brother from the time I was about nine years old, and I don't have words big enough to describe my sense of loss at his death. The aftermath of the attacks was a difficult time for the country, which we felt acutely in Washington, DC, both because the town was awash in talk of the response to the attacks and because envelopes of anthrax began to turn up in some congressional offices, killing two postal workers and endangering several of my friends who worked on Capitol Hill. It felt as if a threatening, incomprehensible world had arrived at our doorstep, shattering our collective sense of safety.

This grief was compounded a year later, when a sniper began to terrorize the DC area, shooting people at random as they were doing everyday things, like filling their cars with gas, going to the hardware store, or dropping their children off at school. When the sniper was ultimately caught after three terrifying weeks, I learned that he and his nephew had been coming regularly to exercise at our local YMCA, which served as the bus stop for our eldest daughter and the preschool for our younger one. We were at that YMCA every day, parking in the same lot with a sedan tricked out so that a rifle could be fired unseen by someone lying on their stomach, firing out of the trunk. Suddenly, it felt as if danger was all around us, threatening my country and looming over my girls. Those years of my life were enshrouded in a dark cloud of grief and fear.

When I am uneasy, I look for things to read. I try to find comfort from information, from attempting to figure out how others have responded to the things that I am struggling with. So as I wrestled with the feeling that there were dangers around my family that I couldn't control, and that I had real limitations in how much I could protect my daughters, I started to explore how regular people coped with the dangers of the times they lived in, beginning with the regular people in my own life. I expected my parents and my mother-in-law, all fiercely protective of their loved ones, to be freaked out after 9/11, but they were strangely much calmer than I was. It hit me that they had endured enormous turmoil in their home countries when they were young, and their parents' times were even more precarious. The sense of being swept up in dangerous events that you don't control was new to me, but it wasn't new to them. I began to understand that turmoil is actually the norm; from the vantage point of human history, it's times of safety and stability that are unusual.

I dove into books about other eras in history that felt chaotic and dangerous, looking for bits of wisdom about how people coped in those times with problems far bigger than anything I have ever faced: famine, war, plague. The further back you go (and I am enough of a nerd that my reading took me back as far as the Middle Ages), the more it seems that human history is an enormous tangled mess of conflict, epidemic, and upheaval in which regular people—particularly women—suffer enormously. And of course, this isn't just true in history books; it's very much the reality in far too much of the world today. Looking for a way to cope with what seemed overwhelming, I learned that everyday people have through the ages shown great courage in the face of the unimaginable. The dangers that were rocking my particular world weren't exceptional at all. In fact, I had been incredibly lucky to have lived forty years without really encountering them.

And those notable people that we all hear about when we are growing up? My reading gave me a new perspective on them, too. I discovered that our heroes are not so shiny after all, which I found oddly comforting. They are more like the rest of us, so maybe we are made of the same stuff. I did another batch of digging into history the year that I took the job in the Obama administration, because the times we were living in felt so scary. The energy after President Obama's election was exhilarating, but the facts on the ground about the economy were terrifying. The country was shedding as many as 700,000 jobs every month. It was like looking into the abyss and not being able to see the bottom. That's the kind of moment that you think of as being a time for heroism, for the really brilliant people—the Jeffersons and Lincolns—to arrive with their superior wisdom.

I had every confidence in President Obama's superior wisdom, and I had a lot of respect for my colleagues on his team, but for all of the brilliance on our staff, we were still a group of people struggling to understand the depth of an almost unprecedented problem, and working mightily—in the dark, it seemed—to build a road map to the solution. It was a time when I wanted to picture serene heroic figures in the room drawing up the plans to save us all. Except, to my astonishment, I *knew* the people in the room making the big decisions and working to implement them. Even more frightening, I was one of them. I knew their flaws and foibles. I witnessed some serious disagreements. Just at a time when you want those polished, shiny heroes of the history books, we had regular folks. Committed, smart, skilled, but still — regular folks. Doing the best they could.

That turns out to be what heroes are: not exceptional beings possessed of qualities that elude the rest of us, but regular people, doing the best they can in trying times. Lincoln came into office just as the country was ripping itself apart. He didn't know how he was going to save it, and he very nearly failed. He struggled, made some brilliant decisions, gave some of history's most eloquent speeches, and made some epic mistakes. He used his war powers to suspend people's rights, a decision still debated today, and he arrived at the decision to emancipate slaves only when it served the purpose of winning the war, not sooner. He was not perfect by any means, but he is still someone we rightly revere, especially because he was so human.

Franklin Delano Roosevelt, another president I greatly admire, famously cheated on his wife, signed an executive order to place Americans of Japanese descent in internment camps, and tried a few end runs around the Constitution. He also brought us out of the Great Depression, created the immensely popular and important Social Security program, and saw the dangers of the war in Europe before the rest of the country, maneuvering brilliantly in myriad ways to ensure that the good guys ended up winning the Second World War. He grappled with a physical disability, keeping it from the public while also creating facilities for kids with conditions like his.

We can admire the heroism of people like Lincoln and FDR while looking with clear eyes at their flaws. More importantly, we can recognize that, in the moment, they struggled. They got things wrong. They felt fear and even despair. The answers were not always clear to them. In fact, what look like brilliant strategies now were frequently a result of luck or accident. In other words, they were regular folks doing the best they could in trying times, which is what the rest of us are, too.

I live in a town with monuments to these people, beautiful public spaces like the Lincoln and FDR memorials, which have their eloquent words etched on the walls and which remind us of our highest ideals and our struggles through challenging times. Although I take inspiration from these places, I take more comfort from the moments when the people they memorialize doubted and struggled, when they made mistakes. That's what makes them like the rest of us. It's what reminded me to take heart when I was in the room with the president's team, grappling with challenges that affected millions of lives, when the answers weren't clear. Heroism doesn't mean bringing superhuman powers to whatever the task at hand is; it demands that you be what you are, human and frail, giving it your very best even as you wonder whether it is enough.

What If the Hero Is You?

> Whether I shall turn out to be the hero of my own life,
> or whether that station will be held by anybody else, these
> pages must show.

Those are the opening words of *David Copperfield*, a novel by Charles Dickens that my dad loved, and that is a sentimental favorite of mine. For hundreds of pages, the narrator recounts the adventures of his life and gradually answers the question that is posed in this famous first sentence. It takes you inside the idea of a hero in an interesting way. What does it mean to be the hero of your own life? What qualities does that take? What does that notion inspire in you?

It surely doesn't mean building yourself up to be the kind of puffed-up persona who gets fed to us in the history books. Rather, I think it means investing in being authentically who you are and recognizing that the qualities that you bring into the room with you are valuable and enough for whatever situation you're in. I can think of no better example of this than the very inspiring Michelle Obama, who, when she became first lady, made a concerted effort to remain exactly who she was, comfortable in her own skin, demonstrating every reason why the world should delight in watching a girl from the South Side of Chicago bring her own particular grace to the role of first lady.

I had the privilege of watching her, over and over, meet with groups of students and young people who idolized her so much that they would scream or burst into tears when she walked into a room. She went out of her way to make the case that she was no different from them because she understood deeply that it was true. She would say things like, "There's no magic dust that someone dropped on me and Barack, there's no special quality that either of us has that you don't have. I come from a neighborhood just like yours. The South Side of Chicago is still full of people like me." Part of what makes her a hero to others is that she shows every sign of being the hero of her own life. She is not afraid to be authentically who she is; she understands that it's enough for any situation, and she demonstrates that any of us can possess those same qualities.

Just as important as authenticity among the qualities that make people visibly the heroes of their own lives is integrity, the gift of having a strong sense of what is important and being able to stick with it despite the distractions and temptations that life sends your way. I think of this as the quality of having your life be *about* something. I have been fortunate in the sense that the work that I do for a living has always been connected to a deep sense of purpose, but I don't think that this quality of integrity must mean dedicating yourself to a particular cause. Your life could be about creating security for your family, being a good neighbor, or showing up with kindness wherever you go. It could be about creating beautiful surroundings, bringing music into the world, or doing your work well, no matter what that work is. There are as many potential purposes as there are people.

Raul Yzaguirre gave me tremendous insight into what it means to live and work with integrity. His commitment to the civil rights movement is deep. His work in the movement started when he was a teen and has continued throughout his life. It was as if every fiber of his being was focused on trying to have an impact on poverty and discrimination in the Latino community. His leadership of NCLR was focused on those things, and he insisted on that kind of focus from his staff. But Washington is a town full of distractions and contradictions, and there were many turning points during Raul's years at NCLR in which he could have lost his focus or compromised his values in exchange for greater security for his family or his organization. The town is full of people who do good work, but who have also lost their way in some way. I witnessed more than one occasion when Raul simply refused to lose his focus, even if it cost him or his organization dearly.

Before I got to NCLR, there was a time when Raul was working to restore some of the federal funding that had been eliminated in the early years of the Reagan administration. He went to a meeting at the White House in which he was warned not to take a position against Ed Meese, who had been nominated for attorney general. He had concerns about Meese's record, and he raised them publicly, knowing that it would cost him federal funds. Then, during the Clinton years, Raul publicly resigned from the chairmanship of a White House task force on Hispanic education that he had helped create, because he felt the administration was using it to put its own record in the most favorable light rather than to elevate urgent problems that needed to be addressed.

Again, he knew that this might cost him influence and even government funding, but he felt he couldn't allow himself or his organization to be used for White House public relations when there was so much work to be done. He also turned down funding from industries that had reputations for exploiting Latino workers, instead offering to help them assess and improve conditions in their factories and facilities. Over and over, I watched Raul make difficult choices because his compass was so clearly set, and I learned the relationship between integrity and heroism.

I see this quality around me in all kinds of less dramatic but equally important ways: in my daughters, each of whom is pursuing work that they love (acting in one case, and museum education in another), even though it means living modestly and enduring periods of uncertainty. I see it in friends who have changed careers, forgoing more-lucrative opportunities for the sake of making a difference as nurses and teachers; and in my sister, who steadfastly cared for our aging dad for a decade while also volunteering at her church. I have tried to follow their example, to have a sense of what my life is about, to feel comfortable with what I am able to contribute, and to have a shot at being the hero of my own life.

Find People Who Inspire You
(No Pedestals Allowed)

Once you allow yourself to understand heroes as normal people, and even to see the hero in yourself, it gets easier to see them all around you. When you're younger, it can be useful to find people with more life experience than you who can serve as mentors, models, and guides. That has remained true for me as I have gotten older, but I also find that I am drawing inspiration from my younger colleagues as well, discovering qualities in them that I aspire to, and finding comfort in knowing that the generations coming up behind me are better than we ever were.

Take for example my friend and colleague Lorella Praeli. She was born in Peru, and at the age of two had a devastating accident that left her without a leg. Her parents brought her to the US for treatments and over time decided to make their lives here. From the age of ten she grew up in Connecticut, excelling in school even as she endured bullying because of her ethnicity and her disability. That bullying turned her into an advocate; out of that adversity, she found her voice.

I got to know Lorella when she was a young advocate for United We Dream, the organization that brings together immigrants like her, who came to the US as children, grew up here, and often didn't learn that they were not Americans until they tried to get a driver's license or apply to college. Her job involved holding the Obama administration's feet to the fire, making sure we were doing everything we could to pass an immigration reform bill or adopt other policies that protected Dreamers and other immigrants. I suppose that means we could have felt like adversaries, because she was pushing, and I was often the administration representative being pushed. But we both wanted the same things, respected each other, and understood that although each of us played very different roles in the conversation about immigration policy, each of our roles was important. If we worked together, we could make progress. I grew to admire Lorella as someone who could be true to herself and to the community she was serving, while also being strategic and tactical, doing everything she can to get to the result she is after for the people she serves. Her compass is set; you can see it.

Lorella's talents were so visible that Hillary Clinton chose her to lead the Latino vote program for her presidential campaign. This put her into the tough world of politics at the very highest level, where she had to work at breakneck speed, make herself heard and understood by campaign veterans who knew a lot about politics but didn't always know what she knew about her own community, and stay true to her compass. Had the Clinton campaign succeeded, Lorella would likely have landed a significant job in the new administration. Instead, after doing extraordinary work for the campaign, she joined the staff of the ACLU, where she led their immigration policy and campaigns team at a challenging time. She and her colleagues have been at the forefront of pushing back on the Trump administration's policy attacks on immigrants, which takes focus, strategic judgment, and more than a little stamina. Amid this challenging work, she took on an intensive nine-week physical training run by the Adaptive Training Foundation, which specializes in helping people with disabilities train as athletes. She decided to redefine her life beyond the limitations of her disability—all before her thirty-fifth birthday.

I'm proud to say that I was there when Lorella was sworn in as a US citizen, having become eligible for a green card through her marriage. By chance, her naturalization process coincided with a ceremony presided over by President Obama himself at the National Archives. I was so moved watching her raise her hand and take the citizenship oath, thinking about how much we as a country benefit from people like her, who work to make this country a more just place.

Deesha Dyer has also become a hero of mine. The typical occupant of the job of White House social secretary is someone with a socialite's pedigree and a political fundraiser's wallet and Rolodex. Deesha had none of these things. It's a highly strategic job, one that requires grace, skill, tact, diplomacy, impeccable taste, and incredible stamina—and she has those things in abundance. In a single week when she was only a few months into the job, Deesha pulled off a state dinner honoring Chinese president Xi Jinping, followed by a full day of ceremonies welcoming Pope Francis, followed by President Obama's appearance at the United Nations General Assembly, which has a lot of ceremony attached to it. It was a little like planning three weddings in a single week—if the entire world were watching your wedding, that is. With the press focused like a laser on the fact that she was an unconventional choice for her job, Deesha stayed focused and performed like the rock star that she is.

That focus takes some serious poise. But what I find even more inspiring about Deesha is that she took on this job, and the spotlight that comes with it, fully embracing who she is and seeming fully confident in what she brought to the task. Her road took her from that firm that couldn't see her as "management material," to community college, to a White House internship, which led to several other White House jobs. We first crossed paths when the education policy team was lifting the good work of community colleges, and she proudly stepped forward to offer herself as an example of the talent they produce. She gave us a great story to tell, which made her a better example to the young people we were trying to reach than all the people with Ivy League degrees that were walking around the West Wing.

For all her tremendous success, Deesha is like the rest of us; she exuded confidence on the outside but didn't always feel it herself. Here's how she put it in an interview with *Elle* magazine:

> From day one, there were moments of doubt: Would anyone find out that my blazer was from Ross and my pants were

from Kmart? Was my hair okay? Was I too fat? Would I have to take out my nose ring? How do I respond to supervisors who are younger than me? Will people find out I dropped out of college? How about my debt? Or the time I was pregnant? Or evicted from my apartment? What if they ask me about politics? I didn't know that much about politics and who was who. As social secretary, these doubts became affirmations of success for me. I became comfortable with being honest with who I was, in hopes that my truth would help someone else or help me stand confidently in who I am.

So many of us feel that we must pretend and that if we end up in situations in which we are surrounded by people whose experience is different from ours, we have to be quiet about our own paths and look more like we belong. Deesha's story is a reminder that belonging is in the eye of the beholder. Her pathway to the White House may have been unconventional, but everything about her life equipped her for her job, and it showed. She's now working at a foundation, giving inspiring speeches, and running the nonprofit begirl.world, which creates opportunities for young women of color to expand their horizons through travel to other countries. All of this while being supremely, gloriously herself.

I met Fatima Noor when she worked for me as a member of the White House immigration policy team. We borrowed her from the US Citizenship and Immigration Services (USCIS), where she was a special assistant to the director. Fatima is a Muslim who was born in Somalia, though her earliest memories are not of her home country but of the refugee camp in Kenya where her family lived in a blue tent in a community with thousands of others who, like them, had fled a devastating civil war. Overcrowded conditions in the camp led to its closing, forcing Fatima's family to make an excruciating decision: while they would return to Somalia in the midst of great danger, they sent her, the youngest, to live with a relative in Denmark in hopes that she could have a better life.

Fatima started kindergarten in a Danish school without yet knowing the language, bravely adjusting to a new life in a strange place very different from anything she had known. Her family reunited years later after her father was able to start a new life in the United States. She proudly graduated from high school and then college in Memphis, Tennessee, becoming a US citizen in the same auditorium where she graduated from high school.

When I got to know Fatima, I was in awe of the kind of strength and perseverance it must have taken for a young girl to separate from her family, start a new life in Denmark, and then start life all over again after reuniting with her family in Memphis. And then something happened that only increased my respect for her mettle: she became the focus of ugly, anti-Muslim media attacks after her college ran an article proudly highlighting her appointment to her job at USCIS.

The articles attacking her were vicious: "With apparently no qualifications other than a few volunteer gigs and a hijab," read one from The Steady Drip, which continued: "Obama has stacked his administration with Muslims—many with nefarious, terror-linked backgrounds and sympathies."

With no information other than her name and a photo of Fatima wearing a hijab, some leapt to the conclusion that she was a shady character with the potential to threaten her country in some way, appointed to a government post she did not merit. The hysterical rhetoric in the articles appalled me. It painted a portrait of someone bearing no resemblance to the quiet, talented, kind young woman who was proudly and ably serving her country on my team.

Those of us around Fatima were horrified to see her attacked in this way, but even as we tried to find ways to support and reassure her, she remained calmer than we were. She stayed focused on her work, reassuring her coworkers that the right thing to do was not to respond to the haters. Everything about her approach to the hate swirling around her conveyed that she had known worse and intended to get on with her life. Fatima is still serving her country in the federal government with the same enthusiasm and spirit that I came to know when I worked with her. She glows with excitement about the ways that her work contributes to making her country a better place. Her fellow Americans are lucky that she is a public servant.

These are just a few of the remarkable women whom I had the good fortune to be around during the years I worked in government. Each of them is younger than I am—young enough to be my daughters, in some cases—and all were sources of inspiration. They are people whose character and integrity I try to emulate and whose example helps me see possibility for myself and for all of us.

Look around you. There are women around you, too, people whom you can draw strength and inspiration from. Some of them will be publicly visible, doing notable things that get recognized, and some will be doing extraordinary things that may be less visible. Look for them, because all around us there are heroes hiding in plain sight.

Chapter 6

DARING TO BE DISLIKED

MY DEAR FRIEND DEEPAK BHARGAVA, A COMMUNITY ORGA-
nizer who led an organization called the Center for Community
Change, has been the source of some seriously good advice in my
life and work. Deepak's life has been about making the world a
better place, particularly by helping people organize themselves
to make change in their own communities. The best advice he
ever gave me is to get your love at home.

Here's what he means by that: No matter how wonderful a
person you are or how lovingly motivated you are in your work, if
you're looking to get affirmation and love from your job, you are
focused on the wrong thing. It's not that these are bad things to
want, or that it's a bad idea for your coworkers to love you. The
point is that seeking love at your job can interfere with the goals
of accomplishing whatever you set out to do. If you're looking
for love in your work, you may steer the wrong course and be
less effective than you want to be. If you have love elsewhere
in your life, among your family, friends, and pets—the beings
who love you for yourself—it's easier to withstand the times when
you have to make hard decisions and when doing the right thing

draws criticism. "Get your love at home" is another way of saying "focus more on what you're trying to accomplish and less on what people think."

For me, this was never truer than the moment I said "yes" to working in government. One of the first emails I got when the Obama transition team announced my appointment to the incoming president's senior staff was from an advocate I have known for many years, someone who does good work lifting the people and issues that often get forgotten, and speaking truth to power. It was a brief note, meant lovingly: "Congratulations! Great news! Now we will criticize YOU!!"

Exactly.

In a way, that email summarizes sharply the dilemma for anyone in any kind of leadership role. You become the principal of a school, and you hope to make a difference. But the moment you're deciding how to allocate resources, knowing that there will be winners and losers, it may not be enough that your intentions are pure and that you have set the right goals. You will have to make decisions, and not everyone will be happy. It helps to know what your purpose is and to understand that this is not the same thing as being liked.

I was taking a job in the government with the hope of making a difference and the goal of bringing to it the kind of experience and expertise I felt were important to inform the policies and big decisions that affect people's lives. I had spent decades alongside many others in the civil rights movement, pushing at doors that had long been closed to Latinx Americans, insisting that we deserved a place at the decision-making tables behind those doors. So, the door is open! There's a place at the table! Walk in, sit down, bring everything you learned with you, and do your best!

If you are guaranteed one thing, it's that people—even people who know and like you—will be angry with some of the decisions you make. And they may transfer that anger to you as a person.

Any time you assume a leadership role in your life or work, it's worth thinking this through: What are you there to do? Are you ready to make decisions that others might not agree with? How much will you let the disagreement bother you?

For someone who works in government, especially in a position that has some visibility, this is a major issue. You can accomplish a lot, but even when you make progress on major public problems, I don't ever expect to see the day when you and your fellow advocates on the big issues can pack up your bags and go home. President Obama used to say that our job in office was to move the ball down the field, to make progress even if we couldn't achieve perfection. He would say, "Even if we can't fix something all the way, if we have a chance at making things better, we should take it. I'll take better every time."

I knew from the moment I accepted the job in the administration that I would have the chance to participate in accomplishing big things and that I would also face criticism when there were inevitable disappointments. That comes with the territory, and it's well worth it if you believe, as I did, that the president you serve cares about the right things and will field the best team to get things done. You know that he will face criticism too, and that his team will be associated with everything that goes right and everything that doesn't. That's what you sign up for.

I also knew when the president asked me to take the lead on immigration issues that I would own and forever be associated with one of the most uncomfortable issues in the Latinx community: immigration enforcement. This is a tough topic for my community because we have a long history of being mistreated by immigration authorities, and the folks charged with enforcing our currently very broken immigration laws often do harmful things. The headlines are full of stories about immigration officials taking children away from parents, assaulting women in their custody, harassing Hispanic Americans whom they mistake for undocumented immigrants, and even deporting people who are US citizens. I had spent a career documenting these kinds of problems and pushing for them to be addressed. Now I would be assuming a role in which I had some capacity to make change. But there's no magic switch to fix immigration enforcement, and I knew that the best I was going to be able to achieve was progress, not perfection. Even if I was wildly successful, I knew from the outset that it would never be enough, and some people would never forgive me for that. Fair enough.

So, I wasn't really surprised when the attacks came, though I was disappointed that some were so personal: "Activists Say Obama Aide Cecilia Munoz has 'turned her back' on fellow Hispanics" (*Washington Post*, 2011). I got called names; my favorite was when a blogger called me the "Latina spokesmodel for Obama's immigration policy." (Spokesmodel! Calling me a token, an airhead, and insulting me based on my gender, all in two words—impressive!) Some people whom I knew and had worked with called for my resignation at various points. Some are still at it, years after the end of the Obama administration.

I learned a lot from the experience of facing constant criticism, some of it from my own community. I feel both tougher and wiser now, and more confident when I must make difficult decisions, including very personal ones. Here's what I took from the experience that I find myself going back to over and over.

Have a North Star

It helps a lot to know what your goal is, and it helps even more if you're clear that being liked isn't it. If you take on a job, any job, from a project at work to running the bake sale for the school jazz band, if your principal focus is to make sure that everybody likes you by the end of it, you are putting your energy toward the wrong thing. In fact, working on being liked can crowd out achieving what you set out to accomplish. This doesn't mean that you have license to be unpleasant, disrespectful, or unlikeable; it means that your job is to focus on getting the task done well, on having a clear goal, and working toward it. Focusing on being liked can get in the way of that. Instead, be the likeable person who is focused on getting the job done well, the person who can inspire a team to work toward your goals together and who gets the project over the finish line in a way that honors everybody's contributions, not the person who gets distracted by wanting to be liked.

Jodi Archambault Gillette is eloquent on this topic:

> I think one of the hardest things that I've had to go through is internal strife within my own community. I mean, I think that's the hardest. That's the scariest. I don't care what anybody on the outside says or thinks about me. I really don't, because for most Americans I'm an anachronism. I don't even exist in this century. I also know that other people have certain ideas and probably bias and prejudice about who Jodi Archambault is supposed to be—about who native people are—that are just really ill-informed and come from a place of old thinking about our level of humanity as native people. So I'm not afraid of outsiders and what they think of me. But I'm terrified about the people in my own community. They are where I get my strength and my resiliency, but that's also where the harshest criticism and sort of betrayal comes from. Nothing that anybody's ever said to me hurts like when my own people tear me down. I think that is something that I try hard not to do now—poke at people who are trying to do something. I always want to send them as much good medicine and good words as possible, because I know what they're going through when the criticism gets harsh.

Jodi's north star is very clear to her, and it shows. When she worked in the Obama administration, she was at the center of a great many decisions that affected Native American people. We made enormous, historic progress on many fronts, but we did not fix every problem; not even close. With President Obama's encouragement, Jodi prioritized, made decisions about investing in areas where we could make progress, and let go of issues where we weren't likely to succeed. Those are hard judgment calls, and Jodi had clear touchpoints to help navigate them:

> You have to just know that you're right with yourself. This sounds very individualistic, but I'm right with myself: the person that my grandmother shaped. I ask myself, 'is my grandmother going to be okay with this?' My grandmothers have both passed away, but if I'm thinking of doing something that they would frown upon, or that they would be sort of shaking their head at and turning away from me, I'm probably not going to do it.
>
> That's my guidance from values built over millennia that teach us how to act and behave on this earth. My grandmothers weren't perfect human beings, but I learned a lot from them and if my grandmothers are going to be okay with what I'm doing then that's all that matters. Everybody else? They're just going to have their opinions. Whether . . . other people support me or not in what I'm doing, or they agree with what I'm doing that's not really important. This comes from really knowing yourself and knowing your family but mostly knowing yourself.

This is getting love at home in the profoundest possible way.

The deepest example from my own life that illustrates what it means to have a clear north star, and to be guided by that north star regardless of what others think, is a deeply personal one. As

I write this, my siblings and I are just emerging from the experience of caring for our dad, who passed away two months after suffering a debilitating stroke a few days before his ninety-fourth birthday. Thanks to my sister, who cared for him with great dedication, our dad lived at home on his own for ten years after our mom's passing, cheerful despite the dementia, which chipped away at his memory, his ability to reason, and his ability to be independent. My siblings and I had long agreed that our north star was to do whatever made it possible for him to be content, which meant supporting him in his home of more than fifty years and supporting my sister as his main caregiver.

Our resolve got sorely tested by his stroke, leaving us with a series of hard choices. Was the care he was getting at home adequate? If we moved him to someplace better able to meet his physical needs, would that shatter his ability to live with some degree of contentment? We had been so sure that home was the right place for him; what if that was no longer true? What will the rest of the family think if we move him? Will they think we are just watching out for our own convenience rather than his best interests? Will they be right?

On one hand, the "what will the people around us think?" question can be useful in the sense that it's a way to make sure you are looking at a problem from every direction, asking the kinds of questions that more-neutral observers might pose, and making sure you are comfortable with the answers. In this case, my imagination put into my cousins' mouths the question that I really needed to ask myself: What is motivating this decision? Which takes you right back to the most important question: What is our north star? What is the right guidepost for this decision? It wasn't what the cousins would think (though as it happens, they were incredibly supportive) or even our original assumption that home was best for Dad. In this case the north star was Dad's comfort, his contentment, and the quality of his care. We were fortunate enough to be able to keep him out of the hospital, which he found bewildering, and moved him to a place where he was lovingly and skillfully cared for. My sister, nephew, and I were with him on his last full day. We chatted, remembered happy times, and watched hummingbirds. He was content. A clear north star was everything.

Decide Whose Feedback You Value and Ask for It

I'm a big believer in asking for feedback in any situation, but it is especially helpful to find trustworthy sources of feedback when you are getting criticized or attacked. Your defensive reflexes can kick in, focusing you on protecting yourself. This, in turn, can distort your judgment, because guess what? The critics could be right. Or maybe they're mostly wrong, but there's a kernel of truth at the heart of their argument that is worth recognizing. The criticism, right or wrong, could be a signal that you need a course correction of some kind, or it could be an opportunity to really kick the tires on what you're doing and reaffirm that you are getting it right. The point is that you can't make that assessment if you are in "protect myself at all costs" mode.

A moment when you feel attacked or criticized can be a valuable opportunity to ask for feedback, but it's critical to identify someone whom you respect, whose views are well informed, and who will tell you the truth in a way that you can hear it. In an extreme situation where folks are shouting at you or calling you names, it is rare that those same people will make good sounding boards. But even when there is shouting, I have always been able to find voices that are equally passionate but less strident, and more willing to engage in conversation and provide feedback that is useful to hear.

At various moments during the Obama years, I was the target of advocacy campaigns because advocates didn't like the way immigration enforcement was being carried out. It wasn't a particularly comfortable experience, but the criticism was about policy and the way those policies were being carried out in an area that I was responsible for, and one that I care about a great deal. I have to say that I didn't appreciate the yelling or the personal attacks, but I quickly learned to block out what felt like unsubstantiated noise and focus on the kind of advocacy that could allow me to delve into the situation in a thoughtful way. It helped a lot that my family didn't flinch when the attacks came; I was getting my love at home, which helped me withstand a moment of criticism at work.

At the time, Pramila Jayapal wasn't yet in the US Congress; she was leading an advocacy group called OneAmerica. She and Ai-jen Poo, who runs the National Domestic Workers Alliance, were among the many people I relied on for feedback because they were passionate, well-informed advocates who could be simultaneously intensely critical and deeply constructive. They were very publicly and very loudly not happy with the administration's actions on immigration enforcement. As in chaining-themselves-to-the-White-House-fence unhappy.

I understood their passionate advocacy, and I understood that they might even be unhappy with me personally. But I also appreciated that they were looking for answers and policy changes more than they were looking to call people names. I didn't fear their criticism; I felt I had something to learn from it. I accepted that for all of my good intentions, there might be things I wasn't seeing or hearing. I needed information from critics of the administration to know how to do my job well. So, when they asked whether I would meet with a group of immigrant mothers who were in Washington to make the case to policy makers about the effects of immigration enforcement on families, I didn't hesitate.

My team and I sat down with women from all walks of life with stories to tell about how the law and the actions of the Department of Homeland Security had affected their lives. They told us what it was like to face deportation proceedings, what it meant to their children, and what it was like to put your life back together after the deportation of a spouse. Some of it was hard to hear, which is exactly why we needed to hear it.

I had a lot of meetings like that, and although they're not comfortable, they're important. I was grateful that people like Pramila and Ai-jen were thoughtful advocates who were able to engage with my team while taking their concerns to the press and to the public. These meetings were vital for us to test whether what we were hearing from within the government was consistent with the experience of people in the community. They enabled us to examine the impact of our policy decisions and make course corrections where they were warranted. They put a human face on the policy decisions in front of us and helped us to see when we were off course. This feedback contributed mightily to the more thoughtful set of priorities for immigration enforcement that we ultimately developed. I turned to people like Pramila and Ai-jen for advice and counsel because, whatever they might think of me personally and the decisions I was contributing to, I knew that I would get an honest view. Their feedback and ability to connect my team to people whose lives were affected by our decisions was essential.

Hopefully, most people won't find themselves in situations in which there are people calling newspapers asking for your head on a platter. I have found that my theory—that it's worth asking for feedback, especially when there is tension or when you are facing criticism—has held true for me in much less dramatic situations.

It can be helpful to identify a neutral party: someone whose judgment you admire but who isn't your boss or even a direct team member; someone who has observed your work but isn't directly responsible for it; maybe someone who is transitioning to a new job or company who can give you some honest feedback before they go.

For example, when Senior Advisor John Podesta left his role at the White House, I made sure to ask him for some time to solicit his thoughts about how I was doing and how I could up my game. He had been President Clinton's chief of staff, had helped recruit me to the White House, and had joined President Obama's team to spearhead vital work on climate change and a range of other issues. He is substantive, strategic, brilliant, principled, and also very funny and human. He had good advice for me, echoing feedback I have received from others that my tendency to be self-effacing can sometimes undercut my ability to command authority and take up space in a room. I took his advice seriously, and it made a difference.

Feedback doesn't have to come just from people who have seniority compared to you. If you supervise people, asking for feedback from them can be a crucial way to glean useful information. In every place I have worked, I have tried to be deliberate about asking my teams whether they are getting what they need from me, and I have refrained from wincing—and followed up—when they have given me honest answers. My White House team was straight with me when they needed me to behave more like the boss than like a member of the team: I was "staffing myself," doing things like setting up my own meetings rather than allowing them to do their jobs and set up meetings for me. When I needed things from them, I would do them myself rather than asking them for what I needed. They called me on it because I was cutting into time that I had available for things that only I could do and undercutting my colleagues in their efforts to do their own jobs. They challenged me when they thought I wasn't fighting hard enough on some of the issues that we were working on, and when they thought I was fighting too hard on others.

I made it clear to the people around me that they were welcome to offer guidance and that I would take steps to follow it when I found it wise and useful. One result of this feedback loop was that my colleagues and I helped one another give our very best every day. Another is that when the criticism came, from inside or outside of the building, I had trusted sources of guidance to help me distinguish what was noise and what was crucial feedback worth acting on.

Be Willing to Adjust

Making a mistake doesn't feel particularly good in the moment, but it can also be a gift that teaches you something and takes you somewhere you might not have gotten to otherwise. The more cringeworthy the experience, the more courage it takes to ask yourself the hard questions: What did I get wrong? What did others around me get wrong that I could have seen and adjusted? Where did we go off course? Why did that happen? What could I do differently next time? What can I encourage others to do differently? The answers to those questions may do more than just prevent the next mistake; they may lead you to the next good idea that you might not have thought of otherwise.

I learned this lesson in a big way when one of the most public debacles of the Obama administration also yielded one of the most fruitful and transformative lessons. In the years between passing the Affordable Care Act in 2010 and the first enrollment period in which people could sign up for "Obamacare" coverage under the new law, teams of talented people worked night and day on setting up the marketplace for coverage. They worked to build an online system for signing up that was intended to be less like the old way of getting health coverage and more like the way Americans have gotten accustomed to ordering shoes or car insurance online. We famously touted how easy this was going to be. The staff had countdown calendars in our offices in the buildup to the big first day of enrollment. The stakes were high. Affordable health insurance was a signature achievement for President Obama—it was one of the issues that had motivated him to run for president in the first place—and we needed millions of people to come forward and enroll, especially young, healthy people, so that the insurance market would function well for everybody.

If you were paying attention at all in 2013, you know what happened. The much touted healthcare.gov website didn't work for weeks after we launched it. Just when we had ginned up public attention and needed people to come forward in the millions, the website proved capable of processing only handfuls of people at a time, if anybody got through at all. It took six weeks and a herculean effort to fix it. Ultimately, tens of millions of people were able to access health coverage.

This experience confirmed every criticism of what's wrong with government. Even when it's trying to deliver something big and important—perhaps especially in those moments—it's slow and clunky and breaks down a lot. As important as it was to get the website working, President Obama and his chief of staff Denis McDonough weren't satisfied with knowing that we had pulled together a team to make things right; they also invested time and energy in trying to figure out what had gone wrong, and learning lessons from the experience that were relevant to making the government run well.

In this case, we learned that the problem with healthcare .gov hadn't been an engineering problem with one project; it was a management problem that affected the whole of government. Government is painfully bad at the kinds of processes that the tech industry runs every day. Think about it: the tech industry has totally transformed our lives, creating applications on your phone that allow you to buy cars or compare refrigerator models. It turns out that government isn't well-equipped to do the same thing. In fact, government is pretty terrible at it.

In trying to do something major and impactful, we had managed to overcome a big obstacle while also proving that the larger criticism of government was on the mark. These insights led to the creation of something called the US Digital Service (USDS), which began to bring the tools of technology—and the processes that the tech industry uses to build the things that have transformed our lives—to government. My colleagues recruited hundreds of talented technologists from Silicon Valley, persuading them to come and do two-year tours of duty in government, Peace Corps–style. These USDS colleagues were organized into digital teams, and I played a role in placing these teams—who got special dispensation to dress and work the way they were used to, hoodies! even in the West Wing!—with federal agencies who were trying to solve particularly thorny problems.

When we could convince a federal agency to take on a digital team, the results were amazing. I watched as they transformed our plans for a college scorecard, taking what would have become a static website into a release of data that is still being used in dozens of innovative ways by millions of people. A small digital team modernized the process for applying for citizenship and for adjudicating those applications, saving the government huge sums that normally go to outside contractors. Another team helped make the process for resettling refugees more efficient, allowing the government to serve 10,000 more people than anticipated without costing an additional cent. The USDS team at the Veterans Administration began to transform the way veterans receive services—one of the most sacred jobs in government.

Once the federal agencies began to understand what a digital team could accomplish, the demand for their help began to skyrocket. We have a long way to go if government is going to be as effective as people deserve, but in those years, I experienced what it takes to do better. What I saw as the USDS did its work so impressed me that it ultimately changed the direction of my own career. I now work at an organization called New America on a project that is bringing the tools of technology to help governments and community organizations solve problems and better serve people.

I am a person who believes in the power of government to do good. At its best, it's the mechanism through which we as a society protect ourselves and one another and provide the means to achieve our aspirations. At the same time, this experience taught me that the critics of government have a point and that there are lessons to be learned from what we don't do well.

Your failures, particularly the embarrassing ones that rightfully earn you some criticism, can have enormous value. They may teach you something that helps you get to somewhere better. The creation of the USDS out of the stumbles of healthcare.gov shows how the Obama administration took a moment of failure and intense criticism and learned some lessons that we put to good use.

For myself, I learned personal lessons that were just as valuable from the experience of being attacked personally and publicly while I worked in the White House. It took me some time to distinguish what was substantive and valuable about that criticism, and to separate it from what was inaccurate or purely emotional, but in the end, I think I was able to focus on the truths in what the advocacy community was communicating about immigration enforcement, and that information helped us do a much better job over time as a result.

For example, as good as our intentions were about setting clear priorities for immigration enforcement, our initial attempts to focus deportations on people with criminal convictions were too slow and tentative. We adjusted, but we adjusted slowly, and it took much too long to convince the people in the enforcement bureaucracy that the rules we were trying to establish were the right law enforcement priorities. We were slow to make them stick. When we were faced with the first major surge of unaccompanied migrant children at the South Texas border, we were so focused on managing that situation that we were slow to understand the refugee crisis that was unfolding in Central America. We detained families on the theory that detention would discourage migrants from undertaking the dangerous journey across Mexico. DHS Secretary Jeh Johnson ultimately concluded that the choices that we made on the US side of the border had no long-term deterrent effect.

Those lessons led to some important outcomes, including DACA, the Deferred Action for Childhood Arrivals program, which protected 800,000 people who were brought without authorization to the US as young children by their parents and have grown up in the United States. They also led to the enforcement priorities of 2014, which was the first and only time the US government established clear priorities for immigration enforcement, focusing on people with criminal convictions as well as new arrivals—and made them stick. For all the criticism, these are important milestones, especially given the chaos the Trump administration subsequently brought to these issues. If we are going to get to a better place on immigration in some future administration, the lessons we learned in getting to these milestones under President Obama will matter.

Personally, even as I sometimes seethed in anger at what seemed like unfair attacks on me or worse, on the president, I was able to stay focused on my north star of making the best possible judgments in the moment and seeking input from critics with information that could help us adjust course. The fact that

I could go home to a loving family that reminded me of who I am and why I went into this work in the first place contributed immeasurably to my capacity to withstand the tough moments and to ask myself hard questions about whether I was on track. I was getting my love at home, indeed.

I still get annoyed when I get poked by people who insist that we didn't give it our all or that we came to the work with less than honorable intentions, but I have the satisfaction of knowing that I gave it everything I had—and some that I didn't know that I had. I did my best to listen, adjust, and participate in a process that responded to the inputs that we were getting, even when they were unpleasant. I wouldn't trade that experience, or what we were able to accomplish, for the world.

Chapter 7

FACING SETBACKS

EVERYBODY HAS SETBACKS. THEY'RE PART OF LIFE. THE PAPER or exam that you worked so hard on doesn't get the grade you hoped for. The promotion that you wanted goes to somebody else. Your company doesn't win the new client account. The product your team worked so hard to develop is put on the shelf. The ballot initiative that feels like an attack on your family and community passes. The candidate that you can't stand wins the election. Any of these can feel discouraging—even devastating. Over time and hard experience, I have learned that the defeats can be as important as the victories if you keep your mind and heart open to what they can teach you. If you are playing a long game, with a goal in mind, defeats are part of how you get to where you're trying to go. Your job is to make them temporary and to turn them into victories.

The Things You Can Change
and the Things You Can't

Theologian Reinhold Niebuhr's wise and famous prayer is a good guide for a lot of things, including how to think about the times when you face defeat in your life and work. Here's a particularly well-known portion of it:

> *God, grant me the serenity to accept the*
> *things I cannot change,*
> *Courage to change the things I can,*
> *And wisdom to know the difference.*

It is not easy to do any of these things. Nevertheless, over time, I have developed the capacity to spot the occasions when setbacks teach me to double down, do some work, and get to another level.

For example, I was one of those high school students who worked hard to get good grades, signed up for the extra credit assignments, and prided myself on academic achievement. Like a lot of people who fit that description, I felt confident when I got to college. And like millions of other students before and after me, I met my match when I got there, starting with a big fat C on my very first paper. I was shocked. It was the first C I had ever gotten, and it scared me to death.

This fear was compounded by my first-ever college experience in Spanish, which is a language that I spoke at home. Like many Latinx people in bilingual households, I grew up speaking a mixture of Spanish and English, something that few people in my suburban Detroit neighborhood could do. I understood Spanish and spoke it pretty fluently, and as a result, I tested out of the grammar courses at the University of Michigan and into my first literature class. The very first question on the very first day was, "Why is the verb in this sentence in the preterite tense?" I could read the book, talk about it, and understand it, but I was surrounded by students of Spanish who had spent years conjugating verbs, which I had done precious little of. These days, many universities offer "Spanish for Spanish speakers" courses for people like me, to catch us up on the grammar of a language we already speak. But there was no such offering back then. I could talk circles around my classmates, but I couldn't answer the question. And I was beginning to panic. What if I wasn't the hotshot student that I had previously understood myself to be? What if my whole sense of myself was built on a foundation of sand?

Those first weeks of college rocked my world at the time, so much so that I remember that Spanish professor (the very lovely Monroe Hafter) and the name of that novel (*La de Bringas* by Benito Pérez Galdós) to this day. But in the end, I recognize that C and that pesky preterite verb as giant gifts, and that feeling of shock and fear as the fuel that motivated me to raise my game and ask around for help. It jostled me out of my high school–achiever complacency. I got some informal coaching on writing from a friend and found myself a Spanish grammar book. These were setbacks that I could do something about. I was newly humbled, shaken, and more than a little sheepish, but I knew what to do.

The trouble with setbacks is that they don't always work that way. Sometimes the thing that holds you back is a thing you're never going to be positioned to change, and there's no shame in acknowledging it and moving on. I learned this painful lesson early on, when my challenging job at Catholic Charities in Chicago turned out not to be a great fit. The work was satisfying in some ways, but it also involved spending a fair amount of time in the crossfire between parish priests and the leaders of the church. The priests were pushing for more responsiveness to the immigrants in their parishes, and the diocesan leaders were trying to forge their own path without, as they saw it, being at the beck and call of a bunch of rebellious priests.

Because my program was in the news a lot that year, both sides engaged in a tug of war over it. And because this was the Catholic Church, both sides of the argument were being carried out entirely by men—overwhelmingly, white men. (There was exactly one Latino priest in the whole archdiocese at the time, and only a handful of African Americans.) I tried to stay focused on my work and out of the fray, but it wasn't always possible not to tangle with the guys, as I thought of them. In fact, at one point, one of the most senior leaders of the archdiocese sat down to brief me about a major meeting at which men—who were much less informed than I but were more empowered by virtue of being priests—would be making decisions about my work and the people I served. His briefing consisted of telling me that I would be permitted to attend but not to speak at the meeting.

And then he laid out his approach to determine which people to take seriously in any meeting, starting with priests in leadership roles, followed by regular priests, deacons, men, nuns, and finally, just plain women. It wasn't hard to see that I was at the bottom of a hierarchy that was centuries in the making, without any way to rise or be heard.

When it came time to decide whether to leave or stay at Catholic Charities, I agonized about whether I should pursue a role, because being of service to that community meant so much to me, and frankly, I thought I could do it better than the guys. But after a lot of soul searching, I realized that my ability to do my best work there was only theoretical. There were ancient structures in place that would prevent me from having the authority I would need to succeed. This was a situation I wasn't going to be able to change, and I resigned myself to moving on.

It can be useful to make this an explicit exercise for yourself when you face a setback at work or at home. Ask yourself,

"What is in my power to change here? How would I make that change? What isn't within my control, and how much can I live with that?" The first step in facing a challenge is often to reflect and to assess and understand what you do and don't have the power to fix.

Take the Long View for Your Life

If it's inevitable that we will all face setbacks in our lives and careers, it helps to have an approach to put them in perspective. I have learned over time that sometimes it is possible to take the most painful moments—the times when you are passed up for a job or get some devastating feedback—and turn them into opportunities for growth. That doesn't necessarily take the sting out of injustice, like the times when Deesha Dyer and Tyra Mariani were told that they weren't "management material." Their supervisors were not only wrong but might well have been showing some serious racial bias. There is no happy ending that makes that right.

That experience cost Tyra and Deesha some time and confidence, and the kind of employment discrimination they experienced costs women of color millions in lost income over our lifetimes. That's worth fighting against as a matter of policy and justice. But it also matters that Deesha was able to see other possibilities for her life, and that having that vision inspired her to pursue a future beyond the firm where she was working as a secretary and go back to community college, a decision that contributed to her ultimate success at the White House. And Tyra ultimately discovered that she is indeed leadership material. She is a successful president and COO of an organization with a national reputation. They are both living lives devoted to challenging the kind of injustice that they experienced, and I take some comfort from that.

That's part of what it means to take the long view for your life. It means having the capacity to understand that whatever painful moment you're in isn't permanent, but rather part of a trajectory that can take you somewhere else—and maybe somewhere better.

Tyra tells a story about another professional setback, one that she found particularly devastating at the time. She was up for a significant promotion, she was confident that she could do the job, and she was hearing that she was the leading internal candidate. In the end, the job was given to someone else from outside of the organization, and the people above her never told her; she found out through the grapevine. Tyra is a slender, soft-spoken African American woman who looks younger than her years. She wonders to this day whether her "packaging" had something to do with the decision. She says wryly, "You know how they sometimes say that they 'can't see someone in that kind of role?'"

Tyra took the long view. She reached out to the decision makers and asked them what happened and why the decision turned out the way it did. She also looked at her new coworker with an open mind, and she thought about the impact the decision had on her work and her life. "Those reconciliation conversations went a long way," she says. "The beautiful part is that I saw good things happen under the new guy's leadership and realized he had brought credibility that I know I didn't yet have. They made the right choice. That's where my spirituality comes in. From a quality-of-life perspective, this outcome was better for me. Maybe they saw a road for me that I couldn't see. I was relieved. I'm a big believer in the notion that a door shut means maybe that job wasn't meant for you."

Tyra's ability to make peace with an extremely painful setback and see it as part of what led her to other opportunities to make a difference, is the long view in action. She didn't stay in that painful moment; she recognized that it wasn't permanent, and she could see its purpose both for the work she was doing and for her life.

Kara Bobroff tells of a setback in her work that cost her dearly. As she was attempting to open her school, which is built on an innovative model that works particularly well for Native American students, she ran into resistance within a group of allies and friends in the education world. She had to risk relationships, retaliation, and ultimately funding in order to stand up for an approach that she believed in and knew would serve students who are not well-served by the system as it is.

One of her nonprofit partners sat her down and asked her to support an approach and a leader she didn't believe in, and Kara made the difficult decision to step away. She walked away from funding and she put her relationships at risk, knowing that the pressure of going her own way was going to result in increased scrutiny of her school and its results. She took the long view and concentrated on being true to her vision of what the school could ultimately accomplish for its students. The results speak for themselves: more than 90 percent of the students at the Native American Community Academy go on to college.

Create a Ripple

Whether you know it or not, just by virtue of being who you are and making your way in the world, you are creating ripples. Women of color make the economy go and determine the results of elections. We knit communities together and heal them when they are damaged. We are still underrepresented in positions of power in corporate America, in government . . . pretty much everywhere. Far too many of us are still firsts and onlies at the tables we sit at. All of this means that, wherever you are, you are having an impact.

If I have learned anything at all over thirty years about how the world works, it's that progress is frustratingly, achingly slow. Glass ceilings are slow to break; women, especially women of color, are nowhere near getting equal pay for equal work; and there are still way too few female CEOs of Fortune 500 companies. There can be glorious moments when you see the needle moving for people in a way that takes your breath away, like when a bill passes that will mean that millions of people with preexisting conditions will get health insurance. But these moments are vastly outnumbered by the times when we hit brick walls, or worse, watch the needle moving in the wrong direction. Over and over, I have learned that progress doesn't move in a straight line; it zigs and zags in ways that don't always make sense in the moment.

Even big changes that seem to come after a few decades of struggle, like the 1920 passage of the Nineteenth Amendment to the US Constitution granting women the right to vote for the first time, are often the result of longer-term movements that first arose a century or more before. We may learn the names of the notable figures in those movements, the people who made the news like Susan B. Anthony or Elizabeth Cady Stanton, and we may learn about the regular women who organized, marched, and went to jail in the years leading up to the constitutional amendment. But we're less likely to be aware that regular women, whose names we might never know, were organizing locally in 1820, a full century before the change came.

I think a lot about what the injustice of not being able to vote must have felt like to these early fighters, who lived in an era when it must have seemed impossible that things would ever change. They may not have seen how change was going to come, and yet they worked anyway for justice that didn't come in their lifetimes. You must have courage and faith to take up an issue because you feel it and know that it's right, even though it seems impossible to accomplish.

There's a scene that evokes this feeling for me in the 1997 movie *Amistad*, which depicts the true story of Africans kidnapped into slavery who fought back by capturing the boat on which they were being held, and who ended up winning a case in the US Supreme Court in 1841. In one scene, you can see abolitionists marching in the background. In this scene, we are still decades away from the Civil War and the Emancipation Proclamation. The end of slavery isn't in sight, and the pathway toward ending it is not yet visible. And yet these abolitionists with their torches are carrying on work that started well before their lifetimes and would continue long after they were gone.

Think about that: the first public protests against slavery date back to the late 1600s. *Generations* of people fought for a justice that they would never live to see. But their actions created ripples that became waves that over time, after much work, sacrifice, and suffering, combined with courage and leadership among the enslaved themselves, ultimately ended the injustice of slavery. How could you possibly keep doing that work without knowing that you would win unless you took the long view and believed that your actions would create those ripples that would someday become that wave? In our own lifetime, the movement for full civil rights for LGBTQ people, from pre-Stonewall to the legalization of gay marriage, is a huge accomplishment that many thought they'd never see.

I have experienced the highs of getting big things done for people in my career, and many devastating lows, when the finish line is in sight but we seem unable to cross it. I have continued to do the work, and learned how to manage getting discouraged, by taking the long view and remembering that it matters that I keep marching with my particular torch.

President Obama is perhaps the ultimate master of taking the long view. It's how he organized a campaign for the presidential nomination in 2007 that was such a long shot that nobody expected him to win. I got a memorable lesson from him on taking the long view in the winter of 2010, when the DREAM Act came up for a vote in Congress. The DREAM Act is a bill intended to provide legal status and a pathway to citizenship to young undocumented immigrants who came to the US as children and have grown up here. As President Obama likes to say, they are Americans in every way except on paper. I had been working on this bill since well before it was first introduced in 2001. In 2010, it passed the House of Representatives for the first time and headed for a pivotal vote in the Senate, where it had previously passed in 2006 as a part of a bigger immigration reform bill. In theory, it should have had the votes, because eleven Republicans in the Senate had voted for it before; some had even been sponsors of the bill. We didn't need all of them, but we got only three, and we lost by five votes.

This was a devastating loss. Everyone I know who had ever worked on the DREAM Act, including the Obama administration team, gave it everything we had. We held press conferences with unusual allies, like sheriffs, business owners, and faith leaders, to show the broad range of support for the bill across party lines, and engaged most of the president's cabinet in making the case, from the secretary of education to the Department of Defense.

Most importantly, the DREAMers themselves mobilized, made phone calls, came to Congress, and bravely told their stories. When the vote finally came in December 2010, a large group of DREAMers sat in the gallery of seats overlooking the Senate floor holding hands. It was a Saturday, and the White House team that had been working day and night to get the votes for the DREAM Act was gathered in my office on the second floor of the West Wing along with the team working on the bill to repeal the practice of "don't ask, don't tell" in the military. Winning that vote would be a civil rights milestone because it would allow LGBTQ Americans to serve openly in the military. Both teams were watching the votes on C-SPAN and cheered when the Don't Ask, Don't Tell Repeal Act passed, even as our stomachs churned knowing that the DREAM Act vote was next. The cheers became tears as we watched Republican senators who had once been supporters point their thumbs down as the Senate clerk counted their votes, bringing us to a bitter defeat.

Valerie Jarrett's office was next to mine, and she must have signaled to the president that his team was struggling with this loss, because he came upstairs and joined us as we were wiping our eyes. He was clearly disappointed, but he was also calm, almost stern, as he reminded us that it had taken seventeen years to achieve the victory to repeal Don't Ask, Don't Tell. Like every other civil rights victory, the path to this triumph was littered with defeats, with moments when success seemed impossible. He said something like, "This is one of those defeats on that road. But don't ever doubt that the road leads to victory and that what you did will help us get there."

I believe him. And the reason that I can believe him after many painful setbacks is because I have developed the capacity to take the long view and remember that sometimes the ripple we make has long-term effects that we can't see from where we are.

It's only possible to take the long view if you have the capacity to step back and see the broad landscape, including the destination, rather than seeing only the obstacle that is right in front of you. And sometimes the necessity of getting past that obstacle, of finding a way to move it or get around it, gives you the strategy and the ability to finally accomplish the goal. Sometimes the small ripple that you start really is the way that change happens over time.

Find Joy in the Work

You are already working to bring change to the world, just by virtue of who you are, doing what you do. Very probably, you would have liked to have had fewer obstacles and more support in your education and your career and would like to see more women of color succeeding in all walks of life. All of this requires social change. Whether you are doing the work of social change in your profession, or as a sideline, or just by virtue of your own achievements, you are in the fight. And it can be hard and discouraging, especially when there are setbacks.

One of the hardest and most profound lessons I have learned over the course of the many disappointments that come over thirty years has been to find joy in the fight, even when you lose. This work feels personal to me. After a loss like the DREAM Act vote, I don't just read about the people whose hopes have been dashed and lives derailed; some of them are people I know. They are friends and colleagues. There have been times when the people on the losing side of a legislative battle are my family, and it's hard not to take those kinds of defeats personally, because they are personal to me.

But I had the privilege to work with Senator Ted Kennedy, who spent a lifetime in the Senate fighting for civil rights and humane immigration policy among many other things. His record of accomplishment was vast, but he lost many more battles than he won over his decades in the Senate, and if he were still with us, I believe he would say that most of his victories were not as broad as he wanted them to be. From him I learned that it is important to take joy in the fight, because working to make your country a better place—or your state, city, community, or your own organization—is a joyful thing. And allowing yourself to feel that joy is what sustains you over a lifetime. Especially when you struggle. Especially when you lose.

That's why Senator Kennedy threw an impromptu party the day of the biggest legislative defeat of my life, which was the summer day in 2007 when the immigration reform bill failed in the Senate. The bill was the product of a debate that had started in

2000, got derailed after 9/11, and then worked its slow path toward a successful Senate vote in 2006. It would update our immigration system in many ways, including providing a long pathway to citizenship so that undocumented immigrants with roots in the US could apply to get on the right side of the law and eventually become US citizens. The way seemed clear: we would try again, win again in the Senate, and take the momentum through the House of Representatives and onward to the president's desk.

It didn't work out that way, for a lot of reasons that still plague the immigration debate. Despite two decades of struggle, this particular job remains undone. Republican senators who were privately for the bill—I spoke to some that very day—were worried about political backlash back home if they voted yes, even though polls showed that as many as 85 percent of Americans were in favor. So even though they had voted yes only a year earlier, they reversed themselves, and the bill failed spectacularly, along with the hopes of millions of people left with no choice but to continue to live in the shadows. The community of people who had been working on this issue for years was crushed.

And then we got the word by email: Come and meet at a restaurant downtown. "There will be food and drinks courtesy of Senator Kennedy." And sure enough, even as there were hugs and tears, there were toasts and there was even laughter. I was confused by it at first because my feelings were so raw, but after a time, I began to understand.

Doing your part—in your work, family, neighborhood, or church—whatever it is, it's a joyful thing.

You are of course focused on succeeding, and the results matter, but it doesn't always happen, even when you give it your all. There are forces of history that you don't control. But where would we be if we got discouraged and gave up? Where would we be if those suffragists and abolitionists or gay rights advocates who were fighting well before their movements got to the finish line got disgusted with their lack of progress and moved on to something else? We want to be the wave that carries the issue to victory, but what if we are the early ripples instead? We live in a society where we get to try, and the very act of trying is an expression of faith that things can be different. Win or lose, there's joy in trying and in creating the ripple that we believe will one day become the wave that changes everything.

When All Else Fails, Stay Focused on Something Bigger

Some setbacks are personal. Taking the long view isn't just about the arc of history. It can be about the arc of your life, or even a phase of your life; the arc of a friendship, of your college years, a significant relationship, your early adulthood, your shift from one career to another. We will all have professional setbacks, and we will also have personal ones, ones that may rock us to our very core.

I consider myself a lucky person, but my life has had setbacks like every life, including bad breakups, injuries, and lost friendships. When I was in my twenties, my mom was diagnosed with the breast cancer that ultimately took her from us. My second pregnancy ended in an excruciatingly silent, heartbeat-free sonogram at twenty weeks. I'm currently grieving my dad's passing and the pain of saying goodbye to the only family home I remember. In its own way, each of these experiences has shaken me down to my foundations.

I have not found it easy to take the long view in these situations, and while I consider myself a person of faith, I haven't always been able to access the comfort that faith offers in times of loss. What I can say is that I approached these times in my life in a way that will look familiar to you, because it shows up all over this book, not just in my own stories but in those of the women I spoke with who faced their own challenges: I got to work.

It's not an easy thing to describe what that means exactly, and I think it might mean something different for everyone, but for me, getting to work when my life has been turned upside down means starting with my head. That helps me get a handle on what I'm struggling with, which in turn allows my heart the space to do its part of the job. Nerd that I am, that means I usually start processing something hard by reading. I read about breast cancer, about pregnancy loss, about grief, about impermanence. That gives me a foothold, a way to understand my experience and put it in context, a way of accepting that my strong feelings are entirely appropriate.

That foothold usually gives me access to something larger, some way to understand my struggle as part of a larger arena where I encounter others who have undertaken a journey like mine. I'm not the only woman who lost a mom to breast cancer, though my pain is particular, and I still miss her every day. There's comfort, though, in not being alone. Pregnancy loss turns out to be a common experience, except that we rarely talk about it. Learning that it's not so unusual didn't take away the sadness, but it did give me more tools to cope with it and to take joy in the family that I was lucky enough to have.

More importantly, all these struggles, while big for me in my life, are the stuff of what makes us human. There's not a soul on Earth from any country or culture who doesn't confront these hard things. Putting myself in the presence of all of that, and all the wisdom that has been generated across cultures over generations, is not just comforting, it's a source of resilience and strength. We endure these times of trial. They become part of us, and we take them, and what we learned from them, with us wherever we go. They make us more compassionate humans, and perhaps stronger ones. We are part of something larger, and sometimes it is our trials that remind us of that.

We live through eras of personal turmoil and eras of social turmoil. I write this at a time when the setbacks that we face as a society seem enormous. We live in a time of extraordinary challenge, when many of the evils that we have fought throughout our history—racism, misogyny, violence, and economic inequality—are on the rise. While these are not new challenges, many of us will associate them particularly with the era of the Trump presidency, and many of us will recall the night that he was elected as an earth-shattering, stunning defeat. It certainly felt that way in the Obama White House. As painful as that memory is, this was also a moment I will remember as a tremendous lesson in leadership, as the White House chief of staff helped focus the president's team on the larger purpose that was our job to carry out.

I watched those election returns alone at home with a glass of whiskey in my hand. My husband was overseas, and I was worried enough about the outcome that I wanted to be by myself rather than at some gathering of friends watching the returns. Like millions of other Americans, I watched in dismay and disbelief as the results for each state rolled in and the outcome began to come into focus.

Because I was on the White House senior team, I always had an eye on my phone and the email messages coming in. I noticed a message from Denis McDonough, the chief of staff, shortly before midnight. It was terse; he asked the senior staff to get on a conference call. Despite the short notice, we were all on the call, the same group that gathered early every morning around the long conference table in Denis's West Wing office. We could hear the tension in his voice as he thanked us for getting on the phone. "Look," he said, "We can all see where this is going. I understand how you feel. But I really need you to stop watching and go to sleep. We have to start the transition in the morning, and we can't do it with a bunch of really tired people. Please, I need you to get some rest."

That was it; that was the call. I knew he was right. I sent an anguished text to my husband, who was no doubt asleep five hours ahead of me: "He is going to win, and I don't know what to do." Then I turned off the TV and fell into an exhausted, worried sleep.

Early the next morning, my husband called at the hour when I usually got up to send me a hug over the phone, and I stumbled into work numbly, not knowing how I was going to face the day. All of us looked terrible as we gathered in Denis's office. None of us knew what to say, so we were mostly silent. Denis was all business, and even though he had exhorted us to get some rest, he clearly hadn't slept himself. He said something like, "I know how hard this is, and I know how you all must be feeling. Your teams are feeling it too, and we have to get them through today, and through the three remaining days of this week until we get to the weekend so that people can recover a little. I want you each to convene your teams today, and because I know it will be hard to figure out what to say, I have worked out some talking points that you can use."

He handed out a sheet of paper for each of us and then said something like, "Our job now is the transition to the next administration. No matter how you feel about that, it is an extraordinary thing. This country is rightfully proud of its best traditions as a democracy and among the most powerful of those traditions is that we peacefully hand over the reins of government to the next elected leader. President Bush did this for us with real grace and real reverence for the institutions of our democracy, even though he can't have been happy that he was handing power to the opposing party. Our democracy is the most important thing, and we are going to honor it with that same reverence in the way we carry out this transition."

He was right, and Denis's single act of leadership—thinking through to the higher purpose and laying out the very words that we would say to invoke it, knowing that we were too shattered to come up with them ourselves — is among the most moving I have ever witnessed. Its effect on me was profound. I went from stunned numbness to clarity on the nature of the job ahead and the deeply important reason for dedicating ourselves to doing it well: *Right. Democracy. Of course. This feels terrible, but the larger purpose is important, and if I stay focused on that, I can do this difficult thing.* Denis spent the night developing the tools to get us through that day and into the important job we would have to carry out over the following months, and he sent us out to do the same for our teams.

This one moment had a deep and long-lasting effect on me, not just because it gave me the means to get through a really tough day and a really challenging transition but because it gave me an important guidepost for tough times in general. In this case, the higher purpose, the thing we are working to save and protect in the Trump era and beyond, is democracy itself and the values of equality that are vital to its success. Staying focused on that notion has been a hedge for me against descending into bitterness or despair. It's a reason to fight and a call to do it with integrity.

Sometimes we are beset by forces that we can't control. We will all live through eras when the arc of history is bending toward justice, and eras when it appears to be moving in the wrong direction. There will be seasons in our lives when we feel the momentum on our side and seasons when it feels like we have lost it and are going backward. It is in these tougher times when a larger sense of purpose is the most important thing: to know the direction that you want to go, and to hew to the values that will get you there, even when the rest of the world seems to be hurtling the wrong way.

Chapter 8

IN DEFENSE OF KINDNESS

AFTER MORE THAN THIRTY YEARS OF WORKING WITH ALL kinds of people, I've gotten a feel for what my coworkers tend to say about me and how they experience me as a boss, colleague, and team member. And although other people might not appreciate it if it were said of them, I take special pride in the reputation that seems to follow me: I'm known for being *nice*.

I hear this from the people who have worked with me, from those that come looking for jobs because of what they've heard about me, and from others who remember interactions that seemed minor to me but made a big enough difference to them that, sometimes years later, they astonish me with a word of thanks. I have a reputation as someone who is good to the people whom she works with and to the people in her path. This is not just a workplace strategy; it's the way I try to live, and it does my heart good to know that people experience me that way. I credit my mother for my "graciousness" training; she could make even the most awkward person feel at home and loved in about ten seconds. Though I will never be as skilled at it as she was, I have her big heart, and it's gratifying to know that it shows.

I have always thought that kindness makes sense as a way of living life, but I didn't always understand that it could function as a strategy in the workplace until I put it into action. Now I believe that it's a major factor in my success.

Kindness Can Work at Work—But Maybe Not for Everyone

I was going to start by saying that Washington, DC, can be a pretty rough town, but when I think about it, the qualities that make it rough, like the fact that it tends to reward toughness, intelligence, and strength and celebrates what are traditionally understood to be masculine types of leadership, make it pretty much like everywhere else in America. Certainly, it's like many places where people flock to work in the center of the action in a particular profession—New York, Los Angeles, Seattle, San Francisco, Boston, Chicago, Houston, or the new high-tech hubs of Charlotte, Raleigh, or San Jose. We look for qualities like decisiveness, charisma, and courage in our leaders, and although these are qualities possessed by women in abundance, we mistake them for male traits because we are so accustomed to seeing them displayed in male leaders.

Men are everywhere. They are whose voices we hear most often on our televisions and radios, the ones most frequently giving speeches and statements, and the ones we most typically find in political and policy settings and boardrooms, so we associate leadership with what we see them do and hear them say. We don't seem to mind the ones who are a little brash and abrasive—it makes them tough! We think we *want* them tough.

When I came to Washington, which was—and remains—a male-dominated place, I assumed that I should emulate the guys. I even changed my own voice and, as I previously confessed, took up swearing to show that I could be as steely as my colleagues. I adopted their style because it was the only example out there of how to do the work. And I didn't have much in the way of role models who were women, particularly not women of color, who could tell me that it was perfectly okay to be myself. I internalized the notion that to be successful, I needed to go out of my way to show toughness and strength. Kindness and empathy? They were important to me and I displayed them, but I felt I had to supplement them if I was going to succeed.

I now see that I was doing what women in male-dominated fields typically do: we try to act like the men, ratcheting up the qualities that seem to show leadership (I can swear with the best of them!) to balance our "softer" sides, lest we be thought of as weak.

I don't mean to suggest that male leaders can't be kind human beings. Indeed, many of the men I have worked for and with have been big-hearted and generous people, none of them more so than President Obama, who went out of his way to show care and concern for his team. But in my case, there is something about showing up in the world in a short, female body, and then being the sort of person whose natural inclination is to put others at ease, that made me decide early on that being myself wouldn't adequately communicate that I had the backbone people expect in their leaders. I already have a physical obstacle when it comes to taking up space in the room because I literally don't take up much space. Showing up in the world with kindness seemed to compound this obstacle, and I worried about being perceived as a pushover, someone not to be taken seriously.

My concern was not mere paranoia. This actually happens. When someone like me walks into the room, some people really do assume that I'm lacking—in rigor, seriousness, strength, smarts, and leadership ability. While working at the White House, I once got a request from a male governor that involved some follow-up with people at the Department of Defense. He actually asked me, "Are you sure you can handle that? Those guys can be pretty tough, maybe I should be asking Rahm to do this." Rahm (Emanuel, the White House chief of staff who went on to become mayor of Chicago) is famously foul-mouthed, caustic, and abrasive. After one sentence comes out of his mouth, nobody in the room questions his toughness. As it happens, he is also a man with a good heart—and he gets a lot of credit for that as a leader because it feels like an "extra" unexpected quality. It evens him out. For kindness and empathy to be viewed as admirable qualities among male leaders and signs of possible weakness among women is an unfair double standard, but that's what I have experienced, and I have been grappling with it throughout my professional life.

Kindness being mistaken for weakness is such a pervasive and powerful reality that both Patricia Worthy and Deesha Dyer make a compelling case that it's important to show your tough side. For them, being outwardly tough is how you survive as an African American woman in a challenging setting. On the other hand, as Deesha points out, being tough is also often considered a negative trait in an African American woman. In her experience, toughness in a white woman who perseveres may be viewed as an admirable thing, but not so for a Black woman. "You have to accept that people are going to perceive you perhaps in a negative way, but I think that you can continue to be kind about it. But don't be a pushover, because what I found is that, if I was too kind, then people would start stepping on me."

Patricia expresses something similar. As an African American woman who was often the only one in the room, she cultivated toughness as a strategy in her legal and academic careers. "People mistake kindness for weakness," she says. "I wasn't very kind. I did kind things, but I ran my shops tough. Because I was a woman, because I was Black, and because I was young for the jobs that I had, I had to come up with a persona that allowed me to convey that I was serious about things. Because I was so tough, my team didn't have to be. I was the bad cop." Patricia says she remains that way in the classroom. "I am fine with my students having a healthy fear of me. I have always tried to instill just a little fear. If you do your work I will respond, but if you cross me, there are consequences."

Patricia and Deesha are both women with great hearts, and they're plenty tough to begin with. For others, it feels important to cultivate toughness in order to survive and to get the job done. I understand it; I have done it. But it's also an unfair burden. If you think about it, there's no real reason to associate being nice with being weak. Demonstrating consideration and compassion doesn't make a person a pushover. In fact, being tuned in to people's emotions and caring about their well-being can be a source of strength, especially during conflict. It can provide a means of understanding why you are having a disagreement or dealing with a person who is an obstacle to progress. You stand a better chance of identifying and removing the obstacle if you're positioned to understand that person from the inside and able to create a safe enough space for her to share her point of view.

Let's be honest: the culture of many professions, particularly the male-dominated ones, like medicine, tech, law, finance, media, and politics, is that "nice" people are not leadership material. Indeed, it's the rare profession that isn't male dominated, and we tend to think of the female-dominated professions (such as nursing and teaching) as "nurturing" roles. And we pay people doing the nurturing jobs less—way less—than we pay in the male-dominated professions. It's a major thread that runs right through our culture, especially the culture of the workplace. We all find ways to make our peace with it (or not) as we navigate the workforce, but it seems clear to me that one way to begin to change it is to recognize that the "soft" skills that we undervalue are actually assets.

Empathy, for example, can be an enormous advantage when it becomes necessary to have difficult conversations in any kind of job. I can care about someone even when I disagree with them. I can communicate that I am steadfast in my commitment to them as a human being, even when we disagree. That keeps me calmer during an argument, it puts me in a better position to find a way forward, and it provides me with an unshakable foundation from which to do the pushing and reaching necessary in challenging situations. I can convey, "We are having this argument because we disagree on a matter of substance, not because I dislike you, not because you and I have a problem as human beings." Or, to someone I supervise, "I am asking this of you because we have agreed on a set of goals and we aren't reaching them. It's not personal." Kindness and empathy are not qualities that are necessarily about avoiding conflict; they can be a foundation to draw strength from in order to deal with conflict effectively. But Patricia and Deesha are right; you may have to work harder to convey that being kind doesn't make you a pushover.

Empathy Is a Skill Set

The skills that I think of as "people skills"—the ability to read a room, make people feel comfortable, inspire them to be their best selves, and facilitate a decision even when the people in the room disagree with one another deeply—all spring from compassion, empathy, and the capacity to see people from the inside. They are every bit as important as other skills that we are trained to develop and use, like analytical skills or computational ones. Whether you are managing a toddler or a difficult boss (don't get me started on how much these two challenges have in common), it helps enormously to understand what is driving them.

I gave a lot of thought to what made me successful as the director of President Obama's Domestic Policy Council. I'm plenty smart, but I was surrounded by people with much more formal academic training who were acknowledged by their peers to be the best and the brightest in their fields. Some of them reported to me, which can be intimidating if you let it bother you. And I have already pointed out that while I led the White House Domestic Policy Council, I learned that a chief of staff whom I reported to had proposed a couple of certifiably brilliant men for my job and went public with his frustration when the president hired me instead.

Here's what I know: knowing my way around public policy wasn't enough to make me good at that job. I was good at it because I am also good with people. So, for example, when the president of the United States tells you, "I want you to tell me the one policy we should propose to get the most impact for the taxpayer's dollar to create economic opportunity. Where will we get the biggest bang for our buck if we can propose only one thing?" as he did in the summer of 2012, it's not going to be enough to simply have lots of intelligent people on the case.

As you might imagine, in a room with any number of policy experts, you will likely get as many different answers to President Obama's question as you have people in that room. Building those experts into a team, creating the forum where they can debate ideas to make them sharper, and making sure everybody gets heard and can support the final product even if their ideas didn't prevail—those skills are essential, and they are at least as much about handling people well as they are about having good policy ideas. It helps to be able to read a room. You need people skills to move good ideas through a process that can make them real in people's lives. (Our answer to the president's question, by the way, was preschool for every four-year-old in the country. We figured out how to do it and how to pay for it, and even though we couldn't persuade Congress to get it done, we made progress in thirty states. It's gratifying to see the debate still growing all over the country.)

Here's another way to think of this skill set and to learn how to value it: We are told to think a lot about the factors that show up on our resumes, like where we went to school, what we studied, and what professional organizations we are associated with. But a smart employer—one who is looking to build the kind of workplace that is worth going to every day—is looking for things that don't show up on a resume. Lynn Taylor, a workplace expert who wrote *Tame Your Terrible Office Tyrant: How to Manage Childish Boss Behavior and Thrive in Your Job*, told *Forbes* magazine:

> It's the "office diplomats" with strong emotional intelligence who are most likely to be strong, effective corporate leaders. They realize that trusting relationships built on diplomacy and respect are at the heart of both individual success and corporate productivity. An ounce of people sensitivity is worth a pound of cure when it comes to daily human interaction and mitigating conflict. By developing these skills, you'll reduce bad behavior in the office, and your positive approach will be contagious.

Nigel Jacob, the cofounder of the Mayor's Office of New Urban Mechanics in Boston, which is renowned for being an incubator of the kind of innovative ideas that can change cities—and maybe the world—had this to say about the change makers he is looking to hire in *The Commons* (WeAreCommons.us), a publication about innovation put out by New America:

> What I suggest is to hire what I call "hustlers." People who know how to take even a vaguely defined problem . . . and

then pulling that apart and figuring out what you do in response to that . . . We think a lot about emotional intelligence. We see if they can read a room . . . I would choose high EQ [emotional quotient] over regular intelligence any day. I need people who are wise, who understand how humans think and feel.

The longer I am in the workforce, the clearer the vindication of my own experience. I have confidence in the people skills that don't show up on my resume, and I look for those qualities in the people I hire.

Being Kind to Ourselves
When the World Isn't

I am a believer in the value of kindness and empathy on the job, and there is plenty of evidence that it contributes mightily to building teams and workplaces that are successful and good to be a part of. But I'm not saying that demonstrating compassion is easy all the time in the workplace, or in life for that matter. I think of kindness as a hallmark of who I am, but as I write this, I have to admit that I am struggling with my capacity for compassion and empathy while we face so much divisiveness and discord in our country and around the world. I find it striking that the qualities I have learned to appreciate in the workplace have become so much harder to conjure in light of the vitriol that some of my fellow Americans aim at one another and at people like me. How exactly do you apply kindness and compassion at a moment in which people are spouting hateful views—racist, sexist, and even white supremacist views—on the airwaves and in the streets? Is it even appropriate to be concerned about empathy at a time when some Americans are literally under attack just because of who we are? It feels to me like a moment for anger.

As it happens, anger is a big piece of the reason I chose my line of work. In an essay called "Getting Angry Can Be a Good Thing" for *This I Believe*, which was broadcast on NPR and compiled into a book, I wrote about the moment when a close high school friend told me that, in the event of a conflict between the US and a Latin American country, it would be reasonable to move my immigrant family to an internment camp because you couldn't know where our loyalties would lie. That was the moment when I discovered that even people I was close to could at some point begin to see us as "others," people who seemed less than "real" Americans in some way. My reaction to that was—and remains—anger. And I wrote that this feeling became a kind of propellant for my career in the civil rights movement and as a public servant.

I still feel that rage, and it is getting plenty of fuel in this deeply divided era. I feel fortunate that my work in the civil rights movement and in government has given me an outlet to do something about the issues that I care the most about, but I don't think that you have to be a policy nerd to do your part. We can all push back on the things we disagree with in large and small ways, from staying informed and participating in debates at the lunch and dinner tables, to showing up at the Parent-Teacher Association meeting or the city council hearing, to signing a petition, calling your congressmember, marching at a rally, or even running for office.

I'm a believer in taking action, in finding what you feel called to do and doing it, but I also know from deep experience that it can be exhausting. When it feels as if your own community is under attack, even if it is just rhetorical, it feels personal. To me, a verbal jab at immigrants feels like an assault on my family. It is important to pay attention and to do what you can, but it is also true that being alert to every danger, insult, and ugly new policy action can be overwhelming and draining. If you responded to every upsetting development, you would never sleep. It can make you want to throw up your hands and maybe hide under your bed for a while.

I have never quite crawled under my bed, at least not yet, but I will say that my bathtub gets a lot of use in times of turmoil. And I have developed specific survival strategies beyond the occasional soak in the tub as well. First, I have developed something of a throttle system for taking in the news of the day: I absorb it in measured doses a couple of times a day rather than watching it develop all day long. Once I have absorbed the facts, I stop reading about it. So much news gets repeated over and over all day long. Do I really need to focus on it a dozen times? One good dose is plenty.

Second, I notice when I am getting overwhelmed, and I'm deliberate about giving myself space to recharge so that I have the energy for the particular battles that feel like mine to fight. During the time I've lived in Washington, there have been several big moments when women all over the country have come forward to tell deeply personal stories of violence and abuse. I have a story, too—I am a survivor of an attempted assault—and the moments when this issue is in the public eye can get hard for me. I feel both a responsibility to speak out and a sense of real pain and exhaustion when I do. Other survivors have reached out to remind me to give myself space to rest and to share only what I am comfortable talking about. I try to make that same space for the people around me, too, on whatever issue it is that hits a nerve with them, noticing when they seem overloaded and encouraging them to give themselves permission to refuel. These are times that call for kindness, both to one another and to ourselves.

Third, I try to surround myself with people who understand, to whom I don't have to explain my distress because they know. I have the luxury of living and working in communities of like-minded people, which means that my guard can be down, my need to protect myself or explain my feelings less acute. We all have bubbles that we live in, and I am deliberate about cultivating mine.

Find Your Bubble . . .

I think it's fair to say that I built the bubble that I live in on purpose. My husband and I chose to locate our Hispanic and South Asian family in a part of the greater DC area that is diverse, with plenty of mixed-race families, where we don't particularly stand out. Our neighborhood is full of people with progressive views like ours.

That is not to say that everybody on my block agrees on everything—my neighbors are constantly disagreeing on issues like building sidewalks and new public transit routes—but when it comes right down to it, I rarely encounter people whose views feel antithetical to mine in my daily life. At work, at a non-partisan organization that prides itself on honoring a diversity of views, my day-to-day projects largely involve people who are committed to the same ideals that I am. Every place I have worked has also had a deep commitment to diversity. That means I have had the regular joy and challenge of working around people with very different backgrounds than mine and learning from the diversity of experiences they bring to the job, though largely within the context of progressive social values. The civil rights movement I come from is diverse for obvious reasons, and I have learned an enormous amount from that diversity. I chose this life on purpose, and I find that I have plenty of challenge but also plenty of comfort. I have the luxury of mostly feeling safe being who I am in the places where I live and work.

For me, the safety of having this kind of home base has been essential. I think of it as having a strong foundation, a stable home from which to venture out into a world that can be much less welcoming. During my twenty years at NCLR, where we worked hard at being a clear and forceful voice on behalf of the Latinx community in a Washington environment that didn't see us or understand us, it was essential to be able to come back to the office after a day on Capitol Hill and share what the experience was like. I could say things like, "Senator so-and-so complimented me on my English today," or, "I was on a panel with a guy who has such biases about immigrants that he was shocked to learn that my dad was an engineer" without having to explain why such encounters—both of which actually happened—can make you feel tired and disgusted. I was lucky to have a workplace full of people who understood. And I was able to build a circle of friends and family around me that provided that same kind of safety and comfort.

Kara Bobroff, who is both Navajo and Lakota, doesn't think of it as a bubble; for her, it's a crystal:

> Being a Navajo—there are different folks who are called crystal gazers. What they do is look at the top of a crystal, and then at the bottom, which gives you eight sides. The idea is that there are different perspectives that you have when you're looking and concentrating and thinking or praying. So I always try to think about having those different perspectives in my life. They span across gender, and also across race for sure. There are values and perspectives that I look for, and I try to find people who have different experiences and expertise that I can talk to and bring into any kind of decisions that I'm looking to make.

Right now, I would say that the folks that I go to are women. In the last three years, I've had a coach who's Navajo and Chicana and she's amazing. In the toughest times where I have internalized so much stress and pain, when I talk with her, she's like, "You're experiencing racism. You're standing in a room where you're experiencing colonization or you're experiencing racism—I just want to identify that for you." That's been really helpful.

Whether it's a bubble, a crystal, or a series of coaches who know what they are looking at when you describe some of the challenges of your life, it's important to build relationships of safety and understanding.

Not every workplace or neighborhood lends itself to building a supportive community. In fact, our neighborhoods and work-places are often the very places where we are exposed to a wide variety of ideas, different kinds of people, and situations that chal-lenge us, and that can be a good thing. But that doesn't mean you can't also find your tribe, the people who sustain you and give you strength when you need it. Sometimes you can create that network for yourself by staying connected to old friends or family; joining a group with common interests that, say, goes hiking on Saturdays; or building a community garden. Maybe your bubble is a lot of small bubbles. Whatever form it takes, it helps to know where to find your sources of strength. If you don't live or work in a bubble, you can still find one.

... And Then Find Your Way Out

Bubbles can also be dangerous. They can limit your exposure to and experience with the rest of the world. When I worked in the White House, we were very aware that we were operating in an environment that cut us off from the rest of the country. Working for sixteen hours a day in a high-security environment, where your boss can't even go out for a hamburger without a phalanx of Secret Service agents, is a unique experience that is deeply removed from that of the very people whom you are there to serve. The only people who get into the building to meet with you are the people you have invited and cleared through security. Even when you are out in public, the fact of being a White House official seems to make everybody more formal. You are less likely to have a candid conversation because people are either on their best behavior or they are there to protest your presence. Either way, your conversations don't feel particularly natural.

We went out of our way to break through that bubble, to put ourselves in the presence of people with different views, and experiences and perspectives that were new to us, to get out of our comfort zones. The public engagement team did the same for the president, finding ways for him to have private discussions with regular folks, often in their living rooms, when he traveled around the country. President Obama made an effort to read at least ten letters a day from the thousands of people who wrote to him, and the team selecting the letters was committed to making sure he heard from people who didn't agree with him. He responded to a lot of those letters.

From this I learned how important it is to find ways out of the bubble. I have carried this perspective into this next phase of my life, and it feels essential to our national challenge of finding our way forward in this messy democracy we live in.

I have found modest ways of doing this, like going out of my way to find opportunities for candid conversations with people whose experience and perspectives are different from mine. I am in regular contact with people I have met through my work— Democrats who are more conservative than I, and Republicans whom I know from Congress or from previous administrations.

I disagree with them on plenty of things, but I also work hard to understand how they see things and why, and to question my own assumptions as a result.

I try to do the same with people who are not in public life. I took advantage of one memorable invitation from my niece's husband, a firefighter, who invited me to share a meal with his colleagues on a typical workday. His team is racially diverse, a combination of women and men from a variety of experiences and political perspectives. They disagree on a lot of things—we had a lively discussion during the height of the 2016 presidential campaign—but we found more common ground than I expected. Most importantly, I came away with a deep appreciation for how this group of people who disagree deeply in important ways also works as a team, depending on one another for their very lives on the job. They invited me back, and I hope we will have a continuing conversation.

Every community offers opportunities to escape your bubble and form genuine relationships with people who are different from you. As valuable as it is to cultivate the circle of people who sustain you, it's equally valuable to have relationships that challenge you and make you ask hard questions of yourself and your assumptions. Some find this in their religious congregations, through volunteer opportunities that take them out of their neighborhoods and comfort zones, or by simply being open to the kinds of conversations that can happen in the grocery line or at the bus stop. If you are intentional about it, you can find avenues out of your bubble, and if you are open-minded and curious, you may find that you learn things about yourself and your relationship to the world as a result.

I have a greater sense of urgency about the bubbles we build for ourselves and the necessity of stepping out of them, because there is such extraordinary division in our country. I honestly wonder whether we have the capacity to function effectively as a democracy when so many of us seem to be at each other's throats. I thought about this a great deal as I was writing this book, because I was spending a lot of time in the conservative Michigan neighborhood where I grew up, caring for my elderly father as he became increasingly frail. My morning walks around his neighborhood were fraught with a combination of grief at the loss that was coming, my affection for the place where I was raised, and my knowledge that most of my dad's neighbors voted for an anti-immigrant president who believes that the country would be better off without people like us. I was reminded of my high school friend who could picture us being shipped off to an internment camp, and I wondered how to reconcile this place, the people I grew up with and loved, with the real possibility that many of them support a political view that is hostile to our very presence in this country.

I pondered all of this on my morning jaunts, and I also remembered the neighbors who showed up with plates of food as we sat with my mother during her last days. They showed up again as we did our best for our ailing dad, and again after he passed away. I mostly don't know their political views and, frankly, I am afraid to ask. I haven't entirely figured out how to deal with the possibility that the plate of fruit comes from a neighbor who may be comfortable with President Trump's efforts to separate migrant children from their parents or take citizenship away from people like my relatives, who have been Americans for a long time. But I do know that I have looked that neighbor in the eye and thanked her for her kindness and understood that this kindness was real and heartfelt. I know that we have things in common, enough to make us both part of something that feels like a community.

My personal moral struggle is a tiny version of what we are struggling with as a country, and I am playing out in my own small way something that feels big and consequential to me.

After all, what is democracy but a collection of people from very different backgrounds and beliefs thrown together to govern ourselves?

It's hard to imagine that we can hope to move ourselves forward in communities where so many people seem unable to even speak to one another. As angry as I feel, I don't think I can give up on my dad's neighbors, or my own for that matter. It may be that there are some who truly hate what my family represents as people who came from another country, but I don't believe that's true of all of them or even most of them, because I know them.

That's the lesson for me. It's hard to demonize people whom you know, or to hate people whom you have engaged with as neighbors. You can—and should—fight forcefully for your ideals, but if those ideals include valuing your fellow humans, then you must apply that even to those whose views you despise. My dad's neighbors might disapprove of immigrants in the abstract, but my family is not an abstraction; we're an undeniable presence in a community that functions pretty well. We have already been living together successfully for decades. Why? Because we have behaved like neighbors; we have shown kindness and empathy to people who are not entirely like us. I remember that we can do this, because I see that we already have.

Start with Small Acts of Kindness

This is enough, I hope, to keep me from losing faith in my fellow Americans, in the community I was raised in, and the country that I love. It is enough to keep me engaged in a fight for what I believe is ultimately the expression of our highest selves.

I am not naive enough to think that dad's neighbors and I will ultimately agree on all the issues and principles that I think are so important. And I know that some Americans—too many, it seems—harbor hateful views that I can never accept and that I will spend my life fighting fiercely against.

So how do I respond to the evidence all around me that some Americans are capable of doing grave harm to others just because of who they are? I have old habits of using the anger that this invokes in me to fuel my work and my advocacy. But I am trying hard not to be consumed by that anger. I feel it intensely, and it gives me energy and motivation to fight for something better for all of us, for a world where each of us has access to opportunity, equal justice under the law, and the respect of our fellow citizens. But anger is also a destructive force, driving people to say and do terrible things to one another. That's not the force that I want driving *my* actions, or our destiny as a society. It's not who I want us to be.

So, I do small things that remind me to apply kindness and compassion to the people I see in the street, in my dad's neighborhood, and in my everyday life. These may not sound like radical acts, but I have found that being mindful and deliberate about approaching the world with kindness opens me up in all kinds of ways.

I'm the woman who smiles at you as you walk by, and maybe even says "hello" or "good morning." If I sense that you are a person who might be invisible to others because of your size, shape, age, disability, or race, I might go out of my way to say "hello" to communicate that I see you. Sometimes I notice that people walk around with hard masks on, as if they are protecting themselves. Sometimes I see those masks disintegrate at the sight of a simple smile. It's like watching the sun come out.

I am a middle-aged woman, so I know the experience of being invisible on the street. (It's remarkable how we kind of disappear at a certain age—I find it liberating.) After each of two knee surgeries, I spent several weeks walking slowly with a cane, and

I was startled by how many people seemed to intentionally avert their gaze, trying hard not to see the person with a disability in front of them. This experience repeated itself during my father's last illness; suddenly I was seeing elderly people with canes and wheelchairs everywhere. They looked different to me because I could see my father in them. Had I not seen them before? Who else am I not seeing?

My friends with dark skin, hijabs, or disabilities all report the experience of being invisible, avoided, or worse, harassed as they go about their lives. I think about what it might be like to be in their position, and I try hard to acknowledge the humanity of the people around me.

I find this easy to do with some people, and not so easy with others. But if I can find my way to kindness for a stranger on the street in a hijab, why not for the guy in a MAGA (Make America Great Again) hat? It's harder for me—I take one look at him and imagine all kinds of hostility and maybe outright racism—but that means I'm doing exactly what I most resent about what I imagine he's doing: judging based on appearance and hating based on things he imagines. Maybe he feels those things, maybe not. Maybe he's one of the people I have been fighting for, a working-class union member who has been squeezed economically, expressing his rage at the same thing I am fighting, by wearing his MAGA hat. Maybe he's one of my dad's neighbors, or one of the firefighters I met. Even if he isn't; even if he's a guy who can never be liberated from his hatred for people like me, I recognize that if I descend into hatred, I am becoming more like him. I want us as a nation to be better than that, so I suppose I must start with me.

I may have started down my career path because of anger, but it's my belief in the power of empathy, kindness, and compassion that keeps me doing the work that I have chosen. The same force that links me to the people I see in the street, the inclination to recognize our common humanity, is the gateway to recognizing something more important, which is the sense that we share rights and responsibilities in this democracy. We are all in this together, even if we disagree, and we will be more successful as a society if we are doing our best to watch out for one another.

In the end, I think these qualities are stronger than the shouting we all see on television, and the ugly way that some Americans are treating one another. This is as fundamental as believing that light is greater than darkness and love is a more powerful force than hate. If my life in the civil rights movement has been about making sure that all people are treated with decency, equity, and respect, then the anger I feel is not enough to get me—or us—where I believe we should be. That job requires something more powerful than anger; it requires love. It may be that a little kindness turns out to be a powerful force for change. That's certainly how it feels to me.

Chapter 9

FAMILY MATTERS

I'M NOW ROUGHLY THIRTY-TWO YEARS INTO MY CAREER. Twenty-two of those years included the adventures of raising two daughters with my wonderful husband while both of us managed demanding jobs. The struggles of being a working mom have been central to everything I do and am. There were many points at which I wasn't sure I could successfully juggle my family life with a high-intensity job that I care deeply about. This uncertainty makes me a lot like other working moms with supportive partners, challenging jobs, and some capacity to pay for childcare and save for college. For all my particular struggles, though, there are plenty of moms who juggle in much more challenging circumstances, raising children on their own and balancing those responsibilities while trying to figure out how to pay for childcare and other supports on one income. And of course, still others struggle to balance work and life, with or without children.

My story has turned out pretty well so far, in the sense that my children are grown, they seem okay, and so far my marriage has survived for nearly thirty years. But even the stories with the happiest endings include struggles, and my story is no different. For a time, when my girls were small, the demands of juggling work, family, and career almost crushed my marriage. Amit and I made it out of the woods to a much happier place, but there was a time when we weren't sure we would.

The women of color I spoke with have had a variety of experiences with balancing their lives and their families—whether or not they had children—but every one of them expressed what we all know, which is that it's very, very hard. And it's difficult to know in the moment if you're getting it right.

Kathy Ko Chin was blunt about it. "I have had a hard time reining in my drive and fully embracing my role as wife and mother," she confided. "It didn't feel okay for me as a wife and mother to also be ambitious. It is getting easier now that my children are grown. I thought this was just my own burden until my kids let me know how they felt about it. I now start to see that there was an impact on them. Was it fair to them [that I worked so much]? I had adopted strategies, and thought they were okay. Now I feel terrible. The American nuclear family with two working adults doesn't actually work. Extended family situations help. But the middle school/high school years were really tough. There were things I missed."

Patricia Worthy was similarly honest about the challenges and how they played out in her life: "My life is not in balance; never has been. Because I came up at a time when I had to work so hard to do well, I neglected my husbands and fiancés. I'm a little better now, but not much. I would have loved to have had a family, but I couldn't have done it."

It is not easy to offer guidance on how to get the work-family balance right, because "right" is different for every person and every family, and I can't name a single person who believes that they have it figured out. My friend and former colleague Valerie

Jarrett, who raised a wonderful daughter as a single parent with huge support from her own parents, likes to say, "You can have it all, but maybe not all at once." I think she's right, and what I can add to her wisdom is that it's important to know that balance is something that you must seek, and to have your radar going for what is and isn't working in your life.

For me, it is impossible to separate the struggle for balance in my life and family from my identity as a Latina. It's a difficult thing to explain, but culture plays such an important role. We learn who we are and what marriage and parenting look like from our parents. Mine were Bolivianos who were shaped by generations of family and tradition and the heavy influence of their Roman Catholic faith.

A few years after my parents came to Michigan from Bolivia as newlyweds in 1950, my aunt and uncle arrived with their five children. My dad's aunt, who was raising her grandchildren, also moved nearby. There was a steady parade of uncles and cousins visiting us, sometimes for months or years at a time. This was our core social circle, and on my mom's side I am its youngest member, so I had a lot of role models to watch. I particularly loved and watched the women, who taught me everything that I know about being a mom: especially my mom, her sister (my godmother, Tía Mary), and Mary's eldest daughter, Maria Carmen, who had children my age. They were—and Maria Carmen still is—so good at it.

They were traditional moms from that era; their homes were their workplace. Of the three, only my mom could drive (in the Detroit suburbs, where there is little in the way of public transportation), and all of them were amazing. The way I remember it, our surroundings were beautiful even when they were modest, and our houses had lovingly tended gardens. We wore gorgeous prom dresses and school play costumes lovingly and expertly sewn by Mary, the meals at home were extraordinary, and there was always a sympathetic ear and a cup of tea or *cafecito* available at all times.

The moms in my life were fiercely, unfailingly loving, faithful to God, and dedicated to their families in ways that felt rock solid, not just as I was growing up, but throughout my life. The matriarch, my *abuelita*, lived in Bolivia, but she visited enough that we really knew her. She lived to be 102 years old and presided over a family that at one point had five living generations of women. Even now that the older generations are gone, their love for all of us feels like an unshakable, sustaining force. I can only hope to have duplicated that for my children. It is a powerful thing. My Cuban-American best friend, Lisa Navarrete, once described her mother as the kind of person who, if you were in the middle of a blizzard but you needed her for some reason, all you had to do was listen, because soon you'd hear the sound of the dogsled coming with Mom shouting, "Mush!" When you need her, Mom finds a way no matter what. Exactly.

I had a lot of examples of powerful women in my life, but I didn't have a lot of examples of women in the workforce. My own mom is the exception. She was focused on the home—everything about our home was beautiful and done with great care—and she also found home-based work selling cosmetics. Her job gave her some independence and a sense of achievement, but also allowed her the flexibility for her commitments at home, which were her priority. She was insanely good at it, building a sales operation sufficient to earn the company car, in which she drove us to music lessons and play practice. Busy as she was, she cooked every meal; even when she was hospitalized for surgery, she left a freezer full of precooked meals to sustain us through her absence. Once I was a working parent myself, I suddenly understood why you could sometimes find her scrubbing the kitchen floor at 11:00 p.m. I remember with awe how hard she worked and how much beauty she seemed to create all around her.

These were my models in 1992 when, one week shy of my thirtieth birthday, my daughter Tina came into the world. I had been working at NCLR for four years by this point, so I was well established in my organization and in my field, but I was also blazing a trail: I was the first person with a policy portfolio to have a baby. It was such a novel thing for someone in my position to become a mother that, when I made it known that I was pregnant, a steady stream of my colleagues found their way to my office to ask me when I thought I was likely to leave the organization. Everybody assumed that it was unthinkable for a member of the policy team to meet the expectations of her job and raise a child—especially if that team member was a woman.

Some of this was what happened at any hard-driving organization; some of it was cultural. My colleagues seemed to be saying that I couldn't really be a good Latina mom and work that kind of job—which echoed my own anxiety; I hadn't really observed anybody else doing it, either. Could I pull it off?

This was before the 1993 Family Medical Leave Act, which requires all but the smallest employers to offer twelve weeks of unpaid family leave. There was—and is—a law against pregnancy discrimination, but it is neither well known nor well enforced. I wasn't so much worried about the law protecting me as I was worried about living and working with people who assumed that it would be impossible for me to both do my job and live my community's values as a parent. It was striking that so many of my colleagues thought that our boss, Raul Yzaguirre, would not support a working mom on his policy staff, particularly when that mom was covering immigration, which is a high-profile issue. So, rather than wonder whether they were right, I decided to screw up my courage and ask him. I got some time on his schedule and marched into his office to give him my news (which he already knew; as a father of six he can spot a pregnant woman from a mile away and had guessed before I had told anyone other than my family).

I had no idea what kind of response to expect, because Raul's ambition for what we could accomplish for the community is so intense that he drove his staff hard and himself even harder. He surprised me. He leaned forward and said quietly, "I'd appreciate it if you wouldn't share this information yet, but my daughter is expecting my first grandchild, and I have been thinking a lot about the expectations that are put on women in the workforce. Our community's values are all about family, and I think it might be time to put this organization's money where our mouths are." He made it clear that he was willing to figure it out, and he was as good as his word the moment Tina came into the world and remained true to his word when Meera arrived three years later.

This situation opened the door for me to negotiate for the first paid-leave policy in the organization's history. NCLR had very modest unpaid maternity leave that it offered to women but not men. I'm confident that when Raul offered to be supportive, he was thinking about the atmosphere of the office, but he wasn't thinking about paid leave. I negotiated a new leave policy and insisted that it apply to men as well as women. A few years later, I negotiated a flexible schedule. It took me a full year to convince NCLR to allow me to work from home on Fridays, but once I did, it turned out to be my most productive day.

Because Raul had set the tone, and because the people I worked with were wonderful human beings, NCLR became a great place to work for this working parent. If anybody ever raised an eyebrow when I stepped out of a meeting to do daycare pickup or disappeared for a week because somebody at home had the chicken pox, I never knew it. As a result, I became a more efficient, harder working employee, often finishing my workday from home after the children were asleep. I also became even more loyal to the organization than I already was. I turned down several interesting job opportunities because I figured that they wouldn't offer me the flexibility and support I was getting while doing the work of my heart at NCLR. I am living proof that flexible, family-focused workplace policies pay for themselves many times over in loyal, hardworking employees. I stayed at NCLR for twenty years.

Dinnertime and Other Strategies

Having a supportive workplace may be helpful, and perhaps even a prerequisite, but it doesn't resolve questions of work-family balance that may be internal and emotional as well as material and logistical. Especially in those early years of parenting, I was very anxious about whether I could balance being the kind of mom I wanted to be with my work, which also felt important to my family and my community. Like every other working parent, I struggled with the feeling that everybody was getting shortchanged. When I was at work, I worried about what I was missing with my kids, and when I was at home, I was aware of the things that still needed doing at work. I stopped going to all but the most essential events on evenings and weekends, figuring that the networking time I was missing wasn't as important as time with my girls.

I am not going to claim that it was easy. It wasn't. I loved every minute that I was at home with my girls, and I loved my work, but I also remember being exhausted, and shortchanging time with my husband and time for myself. We were pretty good at focusing on the most important stuff: being present for our kids, reading, playing, cooking together, and spending every vacation with our relatives so that the girls would have relationships with our families and knowledge of the rich cultures that make up their heritage. But I was anxious that I was not following the model of the moms in my life, including my own, in achieving the kind of perfection of home, garden, meals, and focus that I remembered from my own upbringing. For several years, I stayed up late on September and October nights sewing Halloween costumes before I figured out that my kids would be okay even if I didn't make them myself. And all this anxiety was wrapped up in a big Latina package: If I wasn't a mom following the model of my own mom, *tias*, and *primas*, then who exactly was I? How could I be upholding the values of the community that I was fighting for if I was falling down on this most important element of my culture in my own life?

Of course, my anxiety about being a "true" Latina mom is only my version of what millions of us go through, regardless of our culture of origin. For me, Latina moms are special because that's where I come from and what I know. But honestly, I don't think I have a single friend with children who doesn't struggle with her version of the same thing. While Latina moms have our own cultural norms (mothering is a central part of our identity, faith is a big deal for a lot of us, we feed people whether they want us to or not, and none of us would be caught dead without Vicks VapoRub™ in the medicine cabinet), every culture has its own version. Judging by my friends' experiences, Irish moms are special, Jewish moms are special, African American moms are special, indigenous moms are special, Chinese moms are special, and so on. We all have our own cultural spin on what motherhood is, and many of us struggle to live up to what feel like incredibly high standards.

One thing that worked for my family: Amit and I discovered that dinnertime was a good barometer for the balance of our work and family lives. If we were having dinner as a family most days of the week, everybody's behavior seemed to stay on track. If we started to slip, you could see it in the girls' behavior and in ours.

So, we moved mountains to have dinner together most of the time, without TV, phones (cell phones were a novelty when my kids were little), or other distractions.

The meals were not even close in quality to those that my mother put on the table. I often joke that my greatest culinary accomplishment is a low-fat vegetarian version of something my younger daughter, Meera, liked on the school lunch menu: it is a kind of chile eaten with tortilla chips called, I'm sorry to say, "chips olé." I won't reveal what's in it, but let's just say it is not something my mother would have served, and it is still a family favorite. We may have been eating a lot of chips olé, but at least we ate dinner together most days, starting with a quiet moment of holding hands and concluding with everybody clearing the table together.

I have since come to terms with the fact that my house will never be as beautiful as my mother's, nor will my garden or the meals that I make. It took years and, to be honest, some therapy to recognize that my daydreams of all the things I would accomplish were out of sync with reality. I chuckle now to think that we bought a house with a substantial yard because I had visions of myself being a gardener like my mother. My friends threw a wedding shower for me that was focused on gardening tools, some of which I hardly ever used. After nearly thirty years, I take great pleasure in looking out at our yard, which has been a disaster for most of our time in our house and has only recently been tamed with the help of a garden service. I raised two girls with a wonderful partner and have been doing my part to make my country a more equitable and just place. I have learned to think of myself as a gardener of things other than plant life.

But coming to terms with whether I have succeeded as a Latina mom in a way that feels consistent with what my own mother, along with my aunts and cousins, gave me, has been a more complicated question. I know for sure that I lived by the most important principle, which is that my girls came first. I chose not to do a lot of things because our time together was a priority. For years, Amit and I barely saw movies, the friends we spent time with were mostly friends with kids, and I turned down job opportunities because I thought they would undermine the workplace flexibility so vital to my ability to be present for my daughters. I developed a reputation as the colleague that you don't bother to invite to happy hour because she never goes. I'm sure I missed a lot, but I knew I was making a choice.

I offer the lessons I learned about my own family's formula for finding balance when I am giving talks to people in the early stages of their careers, and I am gratified to see men asking questions almost as often as women. The balance in my family was possible because both Amit and I struggled to find it. Each of us took leave when our girls were born, and there were no jobs (other than breastfeeding) that we didn't share. But I offer advice knowing that the formulas that work for other families can be very different. At the White House, I worked with men and women who had demanding, inflexible jobs, and spouses at home full-time keeping everything together. During my White House years, our own balance fell apart; Amit did way more than his share of everything, including making every weekday meal and handling all the logistics of getting the girls where they needed to go. I learned from him that love isn't so much the grand gesture on anniversaries or date nights as it is making dinner on a busy Tuesday when you're tired, but your spouse is even more so.

Leaning Out and Leaning In

The lessons from my own family's experience are one example of one family making it work. I have seen lots of other successful families whose strategies are different from mine. I could not imagine giving up a flexible job while my children were little, and I turned down a couple of interesting job opportunities because I feared they would upset the balance we were struggling to build. Although I am sympathetic to the guidance offered by Facebook COO Sheryl Sandberg about leaning in during the early stages of a career, I didn't do it. It wasn't just that I worried about what spending too much time away from my kids might mean for them; it also felt bad for me. I didn't want to miss the precious years of their littleness. I thought of that as I watched several of my colleagues in the Obama administration—women as well as men—juggle the crushing responsibilities of their jobs with little kids at home. They chose differently than I did, and the country benefited from the sacrifices they and their families made. I don't think of them as any less devoted or effective as parents than I was when my girls were small. The point is that every family needs to find its balance, and that balance will look different for every family.

I was so worried about upsetting my family's carefully worked-out balance that I even said "no" to the Obama administration at first. I was holding on to the notion that even though I was not quite following the model of my mom and tias, I was still managing to put my children first. Anything that threatened to upset that balance felt like a nonstarter to me, and I was open about that when the first calls came asking me to consider leaving NCLR to work in the White House. My mother died of breast cancer in April 2008, so when I got the first call that November, I was still grieving and very much focused on my girls, who were thirteen and sixteen at the time.

That call came from John Podesta, who had served as President Clinton's chief of staff and was leading President-Elect Obama's transition. He asked me to consider an interview with incoming chief of staff Rahm Emanuel and his deputy, Jim Messina. I was honest, shared the news about my mother's passing, and told John that I was focused on my family. He encouraged me to interview anyway, and then gave me what turned out to be life-changing advice. "I had children in high school when I was chief of staff," he told me. "It's possible to put your family first, but you have to accept that in a job like this, you get one thing other than work. If you choose your family, then that is all you will do. You won't go to movies or concerts, you will barely see friends, you have to jettison everything but work and your one thing." He was exactly right about that.

I went to the interview because Rahm had a reputation for being unfriendly to immigration reform, and I figured this would be a chance to see what he was thinking. I wasn't hoping for a job, so it felt like a low-risk interview with a good chance of getting some inside scoop on an important subject. I was honest about my family concerns, and Rahm kind of scoffed at that because his young family was living in Chicago and would have to finish the school year and then move, change schools, and uproot their lives, none of which applied to me because my family already lived in the area. Jim Messina called the next day to say, "I know you are worried about your family, so I have very bad news for you: we really want you to be the director of Intergovernmental Affairs." I asked for a day to consult with my family and called back the next day to tell him that I was honored to be asked and would be thrilled to serve in a second term once my children were grown, but not until then. Jim hinted that this wouldn't be the end of the conversation, but I didn't take him seriously. After all, half of Washington was clamoring for these jobs; Rahm and Jim wouldn't have any trouble finding someone wonderful to do it.

The next day, as I was driving Meera to an appointment, my cell phone rang. I looked down and saw that it was a Chicago number, so I took a deep breath, pulled into a parking space, and answered. It was Rahm, promising that this would be a family-friendly White House. Then he said, "Can you hold for a second?" and the next voice on the phone was President-Elect Obama's. "I want you to help me change the country. Hillary couldn't say 'no' to me, and neither can you. I know you're worried about your family; I am too, but we will do everything we can to make this a family-friendly place to work. I will call your husband. I will call your children. I will come to your house; I will make this embarrassing for you; I won't take no for an answer." Really—it was over the top. I learned much later that he tended be shameless in using his considerable rhetorical gifts to persuade people who were hesitating to turn their lives upside down to come and work for him. I wasn't the only one who got this treatment.

I remember every word he said, but I have no memory of what I said. I must have stammered something about how honored I was, and how I needed to consult with my family. When I called Amit, who is usually something of a skeptic, he burst into tears. "You're not just being offered a job; you're being called," he said. I tried to have a calm conversation with my girls about how this meant more bus rides, fewer carpools, and more self-reliance on their part, but they were so excited by the possibility of what sounded like a cool White House job that they readily agreed with their father. I called back the next day and took the job.

I would like to say that everything fell into place and the White House magically became a family-friendly place to work, but that wouldn't be true. President Obama did take steps to create a more flexible workplace. Mostly, this meant that we got laptops to enable those of us who didn't need a high-security connection to work from home. For the first three years, my immediate boss was Valerie Jarrett, who had been a single mom. She told me, "We are going to work very hard, but I promise that you won't miss anything important." She was true to her word, and she gave me the encouragement I needed to walk out the door at the end of the day and make it to important occasions.

But honestly, I was able to spend eight years in the Obama administration because Amit simply dropped everything and took over air traffic control at home. He made every meal (except on the occasional Sunday), did the laundry, took the girls to their activities—he did everything. And my eyes never fail to fill up when I remember that he never, ever complained about the long hours or the stressed-out wife who came crawling home at the end of the day. I know for a fact that, had the tables been turned and I had been the spouse of an overworked White House staffer, I would have complained at least occasionally. The fact that he willingly—even joyfully—made it possible for me to turn myself over to my work was an incredible show of selflessness and generosity on his part. President Obama always made it a point to thank the spouses and families of his team profusely for their sacrifice. He knew what they gave.

Now that my girls are grown, I think I have come to terms with the notion that I succeeded in being my own kind of Latina mom. It helps that I can ask them whether they got what I was hoping to give. Interestingly, our first conversation on this subject happened when one of them found a book that Amit had given me on their behalf one Mother's Day when they were small: *My Mother Worked and I Turned Out Okay*. They found this amusing. They had no idea that he got it for me because I was agonizing about the subject.

I'm including their voices here because, if you're a woman who has children or worries about having them, it might be comforting to know that mine really don't understand what I was so worried about. You'll see that some of our strategies took root, and they noticed. What looked from my end like chaos that fell far from the standards set by my mother, looked very different from their side of the relationship. I would have found it reassuring to talk to the children of someone whose work experience looked like mine. So, here's what my own daughters have to say about it:

Meera wrote:

I don't really think that you being a working mother had as much of an effect on us as you think it did. Until I started attending private school, I wasn't really aware of parents who didn't work. It seemed normal to me; there was no sense that I was owed or should expect more of your time.

The way that the two of you parented was also not particularly gendered, which was a wonderful thing to grow up around. I mostly see that as being lucky enough to have a father who didn't feel emasculated by involving himself in traditionally "feminine" roles, which evened out the burden of parenting and created a positive example for us.

You also both expressed openly throughout our childhoods that your kids were your priority, which really got through. This I'm sure has to do with you two as individuals and your values, but is something that I associate with your respective cultural backgrounds. That always seemed shaped by the family-centric cultures that you both come from as well as what you personally value, both things I really appreciate.

As for family dinners, it never really struck me as something deliberate or pointed, just something we would do if we were all in the house together. It's nice to think that it was something you put real effort into, without me noticing.

And as for your time in the White House, I don't know why you won't believe me when I say that it wasn't a negative experience for me! I was a teenager the whole time, I loved having some space! I also understood, even as a teenager with little to no understanding of government, that the work you were doing was important and that is something I have always taken pride in. It was a pretty amazing experience for me, too.

Tina said:

I think it helped that when the two of you were home, you made an extra effort to spend time with us, and I think that made all the difference. I also really believe that the fact that both of you were doing work you thought was important, and that you included us in those values, had a huge impact as well. We got to see you caring about what you did, and that's definitely shaped the way I look at my own career.

Not only did I grow up learning and believing that men can and should be as much a part of home life as women, but from a young age, the idea that women can be smart, successful, career-driven, and good mothers all at once was normalized, and I think that's so important for kids to learn. I definitely credit that at least somewhat with my own strength, drive, and uncompromising attitude when it comes to expecting more from the men in my life (which I think the world could use more of; men get off way too easy for most things).

As far as you going to work in the White House, I would have hated to see you pass up something so potentially life-changing and awesome in a professional way because you felt guilty about not being as present for us. I think that's a guilt that men rarely feel because it's just expected that career comes first and that the slack at home will get picked up. I'm so grateful we have a dad who was willing to pick up that slack and who doesn't buy into that way of thinking, but it's hard to get over that internalized sense of responsibility as a woman, which I understand, but also resent. I'm so glad you decided to go for it.

There's no clear formula for success that I can lay out for you; there is only struggle, joy, figuring it out for your particular family, making mistakes, and then readjusting. I recognize that it is easy for me to say this now that my children are safely out on their own, but if I were giving advice to my younger self, I would tell myself to agonize less and focus more on having fun. I would say that it's worth having clarity on what matters most, like being there for dinner and bedtime as much as possible, and not being distracted with work or other tasks when you're at home with family. And it's equally worth being clear on what matters least, like the condition of the garden, the magazine-worthiness of the house, or the creativity of the meals. I would encourage my younger self to learn a little earlier that "perfect" is not a visual thing that can be captured in a photograph. Sometimes it's a messy house where an impromptu dance party is taking place, or a heartfelt conversation about what's going on at school over a bowl of chips olé.

Chapter 10

LIFE BEYOND WORK

GETTING STARTED DOESN'T HAPPEN ONLY ONCE. IN FACT, IT'S increasingly unusual to have a career like mine, in which you stay at an organization for twenty years and only change jobs or fields once or twice. If you're a student or someone relatively early in her career, chances are good that the world is changing fast enough that you will someday take a job in a field that doesn't yet exist or use technology that has yet to be invented. Our capacity to be flexible and adaptable, remake ourselves, and change direction is as important a skill set as any other that you will develop. And especially in those moments when you move from one thing to another, it's just as important to consider what you want for your life as it is what you want for your work.

I want to be clear that this last part of the book, the part about getting a life, isn't just for people with children. I think it's a grave mistake to think that the only people juggling work and life balance are the people juggling work and families. It's important to have the time and capacity to just be human—a person with interests, friends, and aspects of your life other than what you do for a living. A person who gets rest, even.

I was fifty-four when I walked out of the West Wing and into the next stage of my life. I had a lot of adjustments to make, not only because I was leaving one intense phase of a career and starting another, but also because I went into the White House while comanaging a bustling household in which two working parents were raising two teenage daughters. By the time I left, my children had flown the nest and my husband had semi-retired into a role that allowed him to spend months at a time overseas, consulting for a project that he cared about and helping to care for his aging mom. I had pretty much never been alone in my house, and suddenly I was on my own for long stretches, months at a time. You would think that, after all of those years of constant work, with only a little time for family and no time for myself, it would be amazing to have a little quiet time—a chance to sleep, catch up on reading, and see friends.

I was terrible at it.

As nice as it was to let go of working so intensely, it wasn't easy for me to adjust to a different pace. I'm lucky that my post–White House job, at an organization called New America, involved a couple of my former colleagues, Tara McGuinness and Vivian Graubard, who both possess the same overdeveloped work ethic that I have. Our boss is another hard-working Obama administration alumna, Anne-Marie Slaughter, who wrote a book, *Unfinished Business: Women, Men, Work, Family*, about work-life balance. She has built an organization that insists on giving its employees the space to do good work without working all the time, and to invest in living full lives. With Anne-Marie's good example and constant urging, Tara, Viv, and I spent our first post-government years coaching one another on how to do things like go home at the end of a normal workday without feeling guilty, stay home and rest when we're sick, and actually use the leave time that we have earned to take vacations that don't involve checking email.

I'm slowly getting better at rebalancing my life, but the experience of making this adjustment has taught me a few things.

Learn How to Work, and How Not to Work

Any stage of your work life can be a stage at which you develop habits, good ones or bad ones. That's true any time you change jobs, set new year's resolutions, or take on a new task. And once you develop habits, they can be hard to break. I find that for me it's easy—too easy—to let the work itself dictate how I spend my days, weeks, and months. This is a downside of doing work that you really care about: everything seems important, even urgent, and it can be satisfying to spend all of your time moving from challenge to challenge, crisis to crisis, without stopping to do important but less urgent things like plan. This problem got worse, not better, when I became a parent. The need to be super-efficient so that I could leave the office in time to pick up small people before daycare closed only strengthened my sense that I only had time to focus on urgent things. In a way, I got much more efficient: no time to talk at the water cooler, lunch packed at home and eaten at my desk to save precious time . . . I got plenty of stuff done. But the cost of focusing on the urgent is often neglecting the *important*, which is a big mistake.

Understand that I was already struggling with this problem when I became a parent in the early 1990s, in the early days of email, before the Internet, the smartphone, and social media changed everything, including the velocity with which we live and work. The challenges are much greater now because we have so much access to so much information, which creates more need to decide what to focus on and what to let go of. At the same time, the very nature of work has begun to change. I know from my experience as a policy maker that the typical wage earner is not doing better now than they were decades ago, and workers are more likely than ever to be in temporary, consulting, or contract jobs, where they don't have the things that should be available to all workers, such as predictable schedules, paid time off, health care, retirement, or other benefits.

That's certainly true for my daughters, who are early in their careers, both juggling multiple part-time gigs that leave them without many days off and no benefits. Their lives are different from mine in many ways, but this dynamic is something that I recognize: we are all living lives with a major need to be efficient, to do what's urgent, and to keep running on the treadmill to get things done and make ends meet.

It may be necessary to be in this kind of cycle to put food on the table and keep a roof over your head. But it's also true that when you're operating this way, you form habits that may be hard to break if you reach a point at which your survival doesn't depend on working long hours seven days a week. This way of operating can be almost like an addiction. It feels necessary, it feels urgent, and it can feel really productive. Your obligations and commitments do the thinking for you in the sense that they form the structure for your day. They may fill your downtime as well, as you slog through the emails and the social media connections that must be managed to keep all your plates spinning in the air. And if I'm being honest, I can also say that I have had plenty of moments in which my tendency has been to connect my sense of worth to how busy I am.

I come by it honestly—I work in a town full of people who are wired the same way. "Look at how much I'm doing!" we think. It makes us feel important. It also frequently diverts us from what matters most.

I made a conscious decision to step off that hamster wheel when I left the White House and started my work at New America, and I consider myself incredibly fortunate that this kind of choice was available to me. I managed to find work that I care about, which I do in an environment in which my colleagues encourage me to get out of the office, to have downtime, and to make sure I'm not just working but also living a life. At first, I set expectations for myself way too high, because I am used to a long workday. But as I started giving myself downtime, I began to notice that my mind was filtering information, making connections, noticing things that I would not have seen if I weren't giving myself breaks from being on the go all the time. Being off duty gives me much better insights that I take with me into the job. I got better at what I do because I stopped expecting myself to be doing it all the time.

There are whole sections at bookstores and libraries full of books that tell you how to be productive, make a difference, and keep it all in balance. It's worth taking advantage of these resources to make sure you find approaches that work for you. If you're interested in the strategies of someone who is admittedly still trying to figure it out for herself, here are the tools that seem to work the best to keep me focused while I'm working, and to help me along the path of not working all the time.

Set Goals and Priorities

A seemingly simple question like, "where do I even start today?" can become not so simple to answer when we have more to do in one day or one month than it seems possible to do. That's why I am a goal setter. It helps to live with an awareness of what you are shooting for in your work and in your life. The goals become markers and guideposts, helping you sort through the zillions of small decisions that you must make in the course of a day or a year.

When I start feeling overwhelmed, I find that it helps to remember what my goals are for that week. If I promised myself that I would get that report written by the end of the week, it's much more likely that I will start my day working on that report rather than letting myself get lost in the endless vortex of email in my inbox. Working on the email would keep me busy, but working on a goal is more likely to be productive. There's a difference.

It helps to walk around with a general sense of what your goals are for the year, then figure out what needs to happen in six months in order to succeed, and then break that down further into three-month increments. From there, you can get a better sense of what needs to happen week by week to stay on track. I try to start each day with some quiet time to remember what's most important, what I have set out to do, what goals and priorities might need to be revised since life rarely turns out the way I expect, and how I'm going to make progress that day. It's not a foolproof method. I get blown off course sometimes by unexpected events, by agreeing to do too much, or by underestimating how long it will take to get something done. But in general, I find that it helps tremendously to have a clear sense of where I am trying to go and how I'm going to get there.

True confession: I am still working on getting as good at setting goals for my life as I am at setting them for my work. I have a general sense of what I want the sweep of a year to contain, like making sure my husband and I have plans to travel together and that we see our faraway daughter often enough. And I'm pretty good at establishing routines that keep me healthy: I have been going to the same exercise and yoga classes every week for years. This is going to sound crazy, but because my work-self is so well developed, I am better at weekdays than I am at weekends. I tend to approach weekends with a to-do list, a set of goals, which is fine as far as it goes, but is not exactly conducive to resting or relaxing. Maybe it's a product of all those years as a working parent, when weekends were as full as—or fuller than—the weeks, or maybe it's just how I'm wired. Probably both. But my new, empty-nest self is still learning how to put "relax" and "stop doing" on my to-do list. Ridiculous as it sounds, it has taken me a while to absorb that resting gets to be a goal. A priority, even.

Find Silence

As I learn how to jump off the hamster wheel of constant activity into a life that is both more productive and more balanced, I am becoming more and more of a fan of silence and giving silence a larger role in my life and work. Some of this is a reaction to the noise all around us. I don't just mean actual sounds, though that's a part of it. I mean that it's hard even to find a setting without some sort of screen producing some form of information that we engage with and process. Everywhere from hotel lobbies to elevators (elevators!), from airports to airplanes, there are screens giving us news, updates on the weather, the latest celebrity gossip, or an advertisement of some kind. Even gas pumps (gas pumps!) have screens these days, ostensibly to make sure you don't miss a moment of news, but of course really to persuade you that you don't just need to fill up your car, you need that giant soda and candy bar that's available only a few yards away.

And let's be honest, we also do it to ourselves. So many of us carry around devices that give us the capacity to engage with friends, play games, schedule appointments, or catch up on the news wherever we are, from the grocery checkout line to the dinner table to (admit it) the bathroom. I'm as susceptible as anybody else: a two-minute wait at the grocery store has me reaching for my phone, and I never lost the habit from my White House years of checking it before I go to sleep and right when I wake up.

I think all this information can be a good thing, and I'm grateful that social media keeps me in touch with the events of the day as well as with family members as far away as Bolivia and India.

But I am also noticing that I do better when I allow myself to shut it out and give my thoughts a chance to wander. These quiet times are when I process information, remember things that got lost in the shuffle, and see things that I was otherwise missing.

Kara Bobroff told me that one of the tools she uses to find balance is her weekly run by the river. She needs the outdoors, some quiet, and some time alone to recharge and renew. Over the course of her career and her demanding work leading a school that is doing pioneering work with Native American students, she has learned that without building in a little bit of quiet, she becomes unable to function.

Kathy Ko Chin told me something similar. For her, the challenge is to turn her brain off for a bit and give her heart a chance to take charge. She says, "I need to quiet my mind, turn off the default, and sit with my heart and listen to it. Grow it. That's my next challenge for myself; I need to listen."

This idea came into focus for me when I stopped driving to work in favor of walking to the metro to get in and out of DC every day from my home in Maryland. I had never done it before despite living a twenty-minute walk from the metro because there were always children to drop off or pick up, or a schedule so compressed that I didn't feel that I could afford the time to use public transportation. During my White House years, it was quicker to drive than to take the train because my work hours took me in before one rush hour and home after the other.

But walking a couple of times every day in all kinds of weather has been a revelation and a godsend. Not only do I get an hour's worth of exercise every day, but I get precious time to think, figure things out, or just let my mind wander.

My biggest worry about starting to commute this way was boredom. I thought it would get really old to walk the same not-very-interesting route a couple of times a day, so at first, I chose a series of podcasts to listen to, thinking that they would keep me from getting bored. They did, but I kept noticing that I was losing the thread of the conversation being piped into my ears because my mind wanted to be on other things. To my astonishment, I badly needed the quiet time. My brain rejected the entertainment and distraction that I was providing it. It's as if my thoughts were knocking on the inside of my head, demanding that I pay attention. The effect has been both subtle and profound. I'm more focused, calmer, more self-aware, and more present for the people around me.

As it turns out, one of the benefits of a little quiet is what you learn from listening to yourself.

Who You Are Is Not What You Do

Perhaps this is especially acute in Washington, DC, and other large cities where ambitious people go to make things happen, but one of the great parlor games in the area where I live is to try to describe yourself without referring to your job. The work that I do is so intertwined with my identity that the descriptors that I use to define myself, right after "Latina," and "mom," are "policy nerd." It feels like not just what I do, but who I am.

There's nothing inherently wrong with being passionate about what you do. I would admire someone who describes herself as an educator, gardener, or musician just as much as I might admire a politician or a famous novelist. But it's also true that the one-sidedness of having work be such a big part of your identity crowds out your capacity to see yourself any other way. In some circles (and there are plenty of these circles in Washington, a town crawling with practitioners of the art of looking over your shoulder as you greet them, scanning the room for someone more important), your occupation is used as a way of sizing you up in the social pecking order.

Ugh. If anything is an inducement to finding ways to describe yourself other than your job, it's that.

When I think about the people I love most in the world, I don't think of them in terms of their occupations. Some of them don't have one. Others have jobs that they do perfectly cheerfully, but which for them are simply how they make a living, not who they are. It would make me sad if I thought that my friends and family described me in terms of my job, even though my work feels very central to my identity.

I think it's important to have an answer to the question, "Who are you?" that doesn't refer to your job. I don't mean a description that you give on first dates or at parties (though that might come in handy) but more a set of things that you know about yourself that connect you to the world in some way beyond the way you earn a living.

If you're a parent, this is easy, and in the most intense years of parenting, it can be hard to find the space or time for anything else. All the more reason, though, to know what connects you to the world other than your children. I am a person who sings, and I waited until my kids were beyond the toddler stage to join a chorus. I might have waited longer if my husband hadn't said to me, "You're a musician, and your children have no idea that this is part of who you are. If you don't get back to it now, you might never do it." He was right, and singing in my chorus is a great source of joy. I took eight years off from singing while I worked at the White House, and I couldn't wait to get back to it. I am always amazed that, after a long day of work, wondering where I am going to get the energy for two and a half hours of rehearsal, I get so filled up by something so simple.

That's the key, I think. Know what it is that fills you up. Understand that there are activities that you engage in—maybe even that you love—but that deplete you. Those are your outputs. Make sure you find a way to balance them with activities that feel like inputs. Time with friends. Time alone. Time bungee jumping. Time with a book or music. Make that part of who you are.

This is about more than having a hobby (though having a hobby is a great way to get input). It is also about knowing what interests you and what makes your heart sing, and building that into your sense of yourself. I have one friend who has a passion for horror movies and another for card and board games. One makes amazing and elaborate cocktails. One of my brothers is a stargazer and a swing dancer. The elder of my brothers organizes the men in his congregation to take hikes in the mountains. My sister helps run a charity at her church. My cousin helps people trace their families' genealogical histories. All of this is so much more interesting than any job.

I learned the importance of all this much too slowly. I was so focused on making a difference in the world and then, after my children arrived, on being a good mom, that I disinvested in any other way of connecting to the world. At one point, a therapist asked me what I would do if I had an entire day to myself and told me my answer could not include any of the things on my to-do list. Not only couldn't I answer her but I was completely baffled by the question. I didn't even know how to begin to start answering it.

I think about that now and wonder why I thought I had a lot to offer in the way of making the world a better place while I was busily hollowing myself out as a person: all output and no input. I'm still wired that way, and I'm still a little terrified at the prospect of a day without a to-do list. But I highly recommend not letting it get to that point. You are worthy of your own time and attention.

At Work, Think About What You Leave Behind

Another antidote for those of us who have a hard time understanding who we are outside of our jobs is a little humility at work and some investment in the people who come after you. No matter how good you are at what you do or how important it is to you, none of us is irreplaceable. And if we think that our coworkers can't get along without us, then perhaps we are doing something wrong. I am a believer in making sure that the people coming up after me are better than I ever was, which is something that I learned from the very best. When I came to Washington, both Raul Yzaguirre and Charles Kamasaki demonstrated the principle of leadership that you should never be afraid to hire people who could succeed you or even outshine you.

Think about that: it takes real confidence and commitment to bring someone into your organization who could ultimately do your job, and in the course of doing theirs, show the world that their star burns at least as brightly as yours does. Many of my colleagues at NCLR fit this description, and both Raul and Charles were generous about putting us all out there, giving us all visibility on our issues, and encouraging us to shine in our work. It's not only a way of making sure good things happen in the future, it's also a reminder that we're not so essential that we can't afford a little time to ourselves.

I am lucky that, during my White House years, it was particularly easy to invest in my younger colleagues because the president inspired—and his team ultimately hired—some of the most impressive young people I have ever known. I am proud to have worked with all of them, and I hope that I provided guidance and encouragement that proved useful across the board. However, I have a special place in my heart for what we came to call "Team Latino" (this was before any of us were using "Latinx" to describe ourselves), which I did very little to organize, but from which I benefited enormously.

We had a few men on the team over the years, but most of Team Latino was Latina. Our ringleaders, without question, were Stephanie Valencia and her successor, Julie Rodriguez, both leaders of the White House Office of Public Engagement and both among the best and most talented people I have ever worked with. We had other great communicators, too, like Katherine Vargas and Ginette Magaña, and extraordinary policy staff, like Felicia Escobar, who led the immigration team for the Domestic Policy Council. We often joked that we taught our colleagues never to underestimate the power of short Latinas: almost every one of us was the same size.

Here's what I most want to convey about this team: although I am as much as twenty years older than some of these women, I have no doubt that their talents exceed mine. It's not just that they are better organizers, communicators, and strategists than people of my generation were at that age—something President Obama remarked upon often, and he is right—I think they are better than we have ever been.

What I mean is that the people I worked with had made enormous sacrifices, like forgoing more-lucrative job opportunities to volunteer for President Obama's campaign in 2008 and his administration in 2009. Some of them were newly out of school, and their first major professional experience was volunteering for a campaign that broke all the rules, invested in the power of organizing people where they lived, and counted on young organizers to convey the message to voters through their own stories and enthusiasm. The result was not just that they changed the world and elected the first African American president; they also learned firsthand what we are capable of in this democracy and that ordinary people can organize to do extraordinary things. This experience changed their lives and their perspectives forever.

As proud as I am of the policy achievements of the Obama administration, I am equally proud of how we achieved them. We were inclusive. We were respectful. We did our best to reflect not only the brilliance and decency of our president, but also the goodness and decency of the people we served. We developed creative ways to engage the public in our work, to honor regular people doing extraordinary things, and we conducted ourselves with honor and integrity. We built teams and we focused on keeping them healthy. I take great comfort in knowing that we have taken these values and qualities with us. The extraordinary people who were part of the Obama administration—including Team Latino—are now working in foundations, corporate America, government, and the nonprofit sector. Some are even running for office. We have taken what we learned into the world, and I'm confident that the world will be better for it.

The lesson for me from the experience of working with this dazzling team was that sometimes it is worth spending the time being a *madrina*—a godmother who sets a nurturing example, who not only supports her colleagues, but also encourages them to support one another. I happen to be older than the rest of the team (okay, in some cases I was old enough to be their mother), but the *madrina* thing isn't really about age. This wasn't just about me supporting people who were younger than me; it was about forming a network of people who supported one another. I got much more in return than I gave, and I hope my colleagues would say the same. It's about finding your people, sending the signal that you should be there for one another, and making the time to make it more than just talk.

I provided three big things to Team Latino while we were at the White House: an office to gather in as a safe space to raise whatever problem or issue they were struggling with, the benefit of experience that they didn't yet have, and the ability to set the example that we should be supporting one another. And honestly, it's not like I had a real choice in the matter; Stephanie Valencia organized us all and put the time on my calendar. I was aware at the time that we were very likely doing something unique in the history of the West Wing; very few Hispanic people have held senior-level White House positions. Before the Obama administration, I didn't need both of my hands to count them. And in the pressure-cooker atmosphere that we all worked in, we could easily have been drawn into a combative competition for attention, primacy on issues, and status. Instead, we formed a team that became a family.

We coached and stood up for one another during challenging times. We used the fact that we all had different skill sets, which meant that we had expertise in policy and budgeting, as well as outreach and communications capacity, to drive strategy and enhance the effectiveness of our efforts, creating a whole that was greater than the sum of its parts. When the president nominated Sonia Sotomayor for the Supreme Court, we added value to the nominations team by bringing our expertise and maximizing the enthusiasm of the Latino community for the nominee. When a bipartisan group of eight senators was ready to start talking about an immigration bill, we were ready with legislative language. On issues as diverse as climate change, education, and health care, we made sure our community was at the table, that our voices were heard, and that people like us all across the country were getting the information that they needed to participate in the policy-making.

What mattered most at the end was recognizing what is true in any workplace, or life space for that matter: we all have moments when we doubt ourselves, when we aren't sure that we are making the right judgment call, and when we struggle to communicate things that matter to our colleagues, bosses, or families. It can feel unsafe to express doubt, to ask the questions that can ultimately help you improve your performance or get to your destination. This was certainly true for me, and I understood that if I was feeling these things, my younger colleagues had to be feeling them, too. It's hard enough to carry those doubts and push yourself to succeed despite them; it's much worse if you feel alone. It doesn't take much to be the first one to say, "This was a hard day—anybody else feeling it?" to create the space for others to express what they're going through. That's how you create a safe space, and once you have created it, it's important to model the behavior you hope to inspire. Ask for help when you need it, and when others ask, listen.

Affirm. Sympathize. Encourage. Coach. Repeat.

The Only Expectations That Matter Are Yours

When you leave a senior White House job, there is a sense that the world expects you to do something ... well, eminent, like lead an organization, become a professor at a well-recognized university (or even a college president), or get a high-paying, influential job at some well-known company. I thought about those things and the sense of other people's expectations and decided to stay focused on what my life was telling me. I landed a job that met all my goals: I found a way to serve at an organization that goes out of its way to make sure you have time to live your life even as you do service-oriented work. I went out looking for work that felt like mine to do and that also left me time for other things in my life, and I'm fortunate to say that I found it.

But as sure as I felt about the work I had chosen, I also wrestled with what I was choosing not to do. I didn't go back to a civil rights organization. I didn't take a job in the immigration advocacy world. I spent a lot of time thinking about what that meant, because these things have been my life's work, and at the dawn of the Trump administration, it was clear that we were entering a period sure to be the most challenging in a generation. My friends in that world were also exhausted, fighting battles on multiple fronts, agonizing over the often-tragic outcomes of the decisions the new administration was making. There had never been a time in the past thirty years in which issues of immigration, civil rights, and economic justice weren't a formal part of my job description. Now I would be working on structures that are important for the work in the long run, but from more of a distance. It felt so strange to make this transition, and if I am being honest, I will also say that after thirty years, including eight of the most intense of my life, it was also something of a relief.

I wondered whether I could square with my conscience that I was taking on a different, more distant role while my friends were engaged in what seemed like constant firefighting, as the Trump administration made disastrous policy decisions that not only undid things that I had worked on, but also unleashed new ways to undercut the lives and the rights of immigrants, people of color, and people who struggle economically. I think of these as my issues; I know a lot about them, and I know a lot about how to fight these battles. Was I bailing on my responsibility to policy issues—and people—that I care about?

Here's why I don't think so: I am grateful to the extraordinary people who have thrown themselves into the firefighting. They are doing heroic and exhausting work, and they are making an enormous difference by doing things like standing up for migrant children whom the Trump administration separated from their parents, filing lawsuits to get the courts to intervene and protect people, and making sure that the media is covering these stories accurately and fairly, lifting the voices of the people who are affected the most.

As grateful as I am for this heroic work, I'm not sure that the advocacy world needed me to be one more firefighter. I think it does need people who are standing back, looking at the larger landscape, and figuring out how we need to prepare for what comes next, and what tools we will need for the work that lies ahead. That's the role I have taken on, and I have come to believe that because there is so much for the firefighters to do, there are not enough people watching the larger landscape.

It's possible that this is just something that I tell myself when I need reassurance that I'm doing the right thing. But I have found ways to stay engaged in the advocacy work as well, providing guidance and strategic advice, even as I go about my daily "big picture" work. It feels like a good balance, and it feels like the work that is now mine to do.

Perhaps best of all, I am, for the first time in my career, in a position to speak with my own voice. During my NCLR days, I spoke for an institution that was representing a constituency. Everything we said was scrutinized by people who disagreed with our work, some of whom were hostile to the very presence of Latinx people in the United States, so we were careful, all the time, to make sure that nothing we wrote or said could be misconstrued or mischaracterized. We never gave our own opinions but spoke in a voice that represented the larger institution and its work.

This was even more true at the White House, where we were always aware that our visitors could walk out of a meeting and say, "The White House says . . . " characterizing even our most minor comments as if they were spoken by the president himself. Worse, there was always a risk that some member of the audience or group we were speaking with would be taping our remarks. And because the Presidential Records Act requires that every form of correspondence—including emails—be preserved for the National Archives, with some communications vulnerable to subpoena by Congress or a Freedom of Information Act request by the press, we were very careful about what we said in our emails. Some of my colleagues were so cautious that they didn't use email at all. Nobody wanted to be the person who made a mistake that embarrassed the president, so we were on our guard 100 percent of the time.

This makes it quite a change to be able to speak with my own voice, to write and say what I really think, because my job at New America doesn't so much require me to speak for my institution as it gives me room to speak for myself. I am trying to use my voice judiciously, writing about policy topics that I know something about and using my voice on Twitter in a strategic way, especially to point reporters and other interested people to information that will help them understand the immigration debate, the Latinx community, and the other issues where I have expertise and a perspective to offer. I also try to have a little fun on Twitter. I frequently hear that people are surprised to see my snarky side. It has always been there, but this is the first time I have allowed it to show in public.

But finding my own voice for the first time in my career feels like it comes with a sense of responsibility, too. It has forced me to think about what I want to use my voice for. If I were willing to put in the work (and put up with the aggravation), I suppose it might be possible to spend more time being a commentator whom you see on television—I do a little of this, but very little, and it tends to be more about explaining policy than about analyzing the events of the day. I'm grateful to the people who put themselves out there as analysts on television because their voices can make a difference. But I find that it works best for me to concentrate on my work, tune out the cable news stations that I used to have to follow for my job, learn what I need to know by (gasp) reading sources that I trust, and use my voice in quieter ways that involve a little more analysis and a little less yelling.

But most of all, in the years since I left government and began to discover my own voice, I have settled on the idea that it's worth being intentional about how I use it, especially in an era in which there is so much commentary on so many things. It feels important to have a sense of how I might actually contribute as opposed to contributing to the cacophony.

And that is what brought me to you—and to this book.

As I wondered what my voice might be for, it hit me that when I attempt to use it in the service of young people, particularly young women of color who are standing where I was thirty years ago, I find that I have something to say that at least some of them seem eager to hear. I didn't have a lot of role models who were women—let alone women of color—to help me shape my path, and too often, the young women I meet feel the same way. I thought maybe a gentle dive into what I have learned along the way might make a difference.

The women I spoke with as I prepared to write this book were frequently the first women, or the first women of color, in the positions that they held. We were often the only women in the room, or the only people of color in the room. We all faced doubt; some of us faced fear; and all of us endured setbacks, embraced courage, and developed a variety of strategies for being tough and being kind. We took different approaches to balancing our lives and our work. We all learned things about ourselves and the world around us in our journeys. Each of us is still struggling in her own way, still learning, and still offering what we have in the best way we know how.

And every one of us feels a sense of hope and optimism about the people coming up behind us.

One of the lessons of my own journey has been how richly rewarding it is to do my part to blaze a trail for the younger women around me and to help them be better, stronger, and more skilled than those of us who came before them ever were. What a blessing to be surrounded by women who make this dazzlingly easy to do.

Please know that what you bring to whatever you choose to do is essential. You are more than ready, and you have sisters cheering you on every step of the way.

WORKS CITED

Alindahao, Karla. 2018. "How I Went from a 31-Year-Old White House Intern to Barack Obama's Social Secretary." *Elle*, January 10. https://www.elle.com/culture/career-politics/a14557984/deesha-dyer-interview/.

Alter, Jonathan. 2013. *The Center Holds*. Simon and Schuster.

creeping [screen name]."Obama appoints Muslim to special assistant in Office of Director for U.S. Citizenship and Immigration Services in DHS." 2015. *The Steady Drip*, January 18. http://thesteadydrip.blogspot.com/2015/01/15.html.

Dickens, Charles. 2004. *David Copperfield*. Penguin Classics.

Fadulu, Lola. 2017. "This Woman Has Been Arrested 131 Times Fighting for Disability Rights—and She's Not Done Yet." *Quartz*, July 22. https://qz.com/1028679/this-woman-has-been-arrested-131-times-for-fighting-for-disability-rights-and-shes-just-warming-up/.

Halperin, Mark, and John Heilemann. 2013. *Double Down*. Penguin Press.

Hunt, Vivian, Dennis Layton, and Sara Prince. 2015. *Diversity Matters*. McKinsey & Company (February 2). https://www.mckinsey.com/~/media/mckinsey/business%20functions/organization/our%20insights/why%20diversity%20matters/diversity%20matters.ashx.

Jacob, Nigel. 2018. "We Can't Promise Them All Jobs After, but at the Very Least We Get Some Work Done." *WeAreCommons.Us*, June 5. https://wearecommons.us/2018/06/05/jobs-after/.

Jayapal, Pramila. 2019. "Rep. Pramila Jayapal: The Story of My Abortion." *New York Times*, June 13. https://www.nytimes.com/2019/06/13/opinion/pramila-jayapal-abortion.html.

Larson, Erik. 2017. "New Research: Diversity + Inclusion = Better Decision Making at Work." *Forbes*, September 21. https://www.forbes.com/sites/eriklarson/2017/09/21/new-research-diversity-inclusion-better-decision-making-at-work/#4bd8cfb14cbf.

Muñoz, Cecilia. 2007. "Getting Angry Can Be a Good Thing." In *This I Believe*, edited by Jay Allison and Dan Gediman. Henry Holt.

Norman, Christina. 2012. "Maya Angelou Public Radio Special: Award-Winning Poet on Why Black History Month Still Matters." *Huff-Post Black Voices*, February 14. https://www.huffpost.com/entry/maya-angelou-radio-special-_n_1276463.

Rock, David, and Heidi Grant. 2016. "Why Diverse Teams Are Smarter." *Harvard Business Review*, November 4. https://www.mckinsey.com/~/media/mckinsey/business%20functions/organization/our%20insights/why%20diversity%20matters/diversity%20matters.ashx.

Slaughter, Anne-Marie. 2016. *Unfinished Business: Women, Men, Work, Family*. Random House.

Smith, Jacquelyn. 2013. "The 20 People Skills You Need to Succeed At Work." *Forbes* (November 15). https://www.forbes.com/sites/jacquelynsmith/2013/11/15/the-20-people-skills-you-need-to-succeed-at-work/#414f032d3216.

Sotomayor, Sonia. 2013. *My Beloved World*. Random House.

Vega, Tanzina. 2017. "It's Time for Media Companies to #PassTheMic." *Neiman Lab*. https://www.niemanlab.org/2017/12/its-time-for-media-companies-to-passthemic/.

Wallsten, Peter. 2011. "Activists Say Obama Aide Cecilia Munoz Has 'Turned Her Back' on Fellow Hispanics." *Washington Post*, November 9.

Wyse Goldman, Katherine. 1993. *My Mother Worked and I Turned Out Okay*. Villard Books.

ACKNOWLEDGMENTS

Four of the women in my life, most of whom don't know one another, conspired to convince me that I could write this book. The first is Jennifer Palmieri, my friend and colleague from the Obama years, who served as communications director for both the Obama White House and Hillary Clinton's presidential campaign. Her book, *Dear Madam President: An Open Letter to the Women Who Will Run the World*, is an inspiration, and a single phone call from Jen when her book was coming out was enough to startle me into thinking that, instead of complaining about the male voices from Obama world—people whom I love, but whose voices are very different from mine—I might consider raising my own voice, because I might have something of my own to say. As it happens, I did.

I had the audacity to share that insight with my wonderful, generous, and brilliant boss at New America, Anne-Marie Slaughter, who immediately believed that I could pull this off, and that it might even be valuable. Her unequivocal enthusiasm was only surpassed by her indispensable advice. I could not have written this book without her guidance and encouragement.

Stephanie Valencia, my former colleague, dear friend, and woman I expect to work for someday, not only told me that I wasn't crazy to be writing a book, but immediately introduced me to her friend Cindy Uh, who became my book agent. Cindy has been indispensable as a cheerleader, guide to the mysteries of the publishing world, and deep believer in lifting the voices of women of color. Without her, there would be no book.

Lisa Kaufman is one heck of an editor, dispensing useful, sometimes-hard-to-hear advice that made this a better book, and Laura Mazer at Seal Press guided me through this bewildering process with a steady hand. Many thanks to Ann Kirchner for a cover design that beautifully captures the spirit of the book; I literally gasped when I saw it for the first time.

I also owe an enormous debt to the women who generously shared their stories and cheered me on as I wove their insights with my own. Jodi Archambault Gillette, Kara Bobroff, Deesha Dyer, Pramila Jayapal, Kathy Ko Chin, Tyra Mariani, and Patricia Worthy—each of you inspires me, and I am beyond grateful for your honest reflections and badass stories. Fatima Noor and Lorella Praeli, thanks for being my heroes and letting me tell that to the world.

I have written that I tend to build families in the places where I work, and those families have given me more than I can possibly give back. Thank you to my wonderful NCLR/Unidos family; I grew up with you and consider myself blessed that the connection endures. Charles Kamasaki generously reviewed pieces of this book and offered hard-won advice after spending the better part of a decade on his own masterwork, *Immigration Reform: The Corpse That Will Not Die*, which everyone should read. Lisa Navarrete and Sonia Pérez continue to be my sisters through thick and thin; Eric Rodriguez, Clarissa Martinez, Darcy Eischens, and Irene Cuyun continue to put up with me for reasons that I can't explain; and I owe Janet Murguía and especially Raul Yzaguirre more than I know how to say.

My Obama family is far too large to list here, but I owe special thanks to President and Mrs. Obama most of all, and to Valerie Jarrett, who was not only my first boss but also became my dear friend. My intergovernmental affairs and DPC teams know who you are. I will always think of you as family and consider working with you to have been one of the great joys and privileges of my life. Thanks for taking what we learned back out into the world; you inspire me every day. Special thanks to Denis McDonough; I hope you recognize some of the leadership lessons here as things I learned from you.

I also have a New America family. I have already mentioned the indispensable roles that Anne-Marie Slaughter and Tyra Mariani played in the development of this book, but I also owe a great debt to my colleagues on the leadership, National Network and Public Interest Technology teams, the Open Technology Institute, and my inspiring colleagues across the organization. When I write about the joys of working with people who are better at it than I am, I'm thinking of you. Special thanks to Tara McGuinness and

Vivian Graubard, who will recognize some of the stories here from our years together in Obama world, and Hana Schank, who gave me the sage advice of a seasoned writer. Emefa Agawu, you didn't have to read the manuscript, but you did, and your suggestions were invaluable.

And, of course, there is my actual family, also too numerous to name, and so fundamental to who I am that there are no words big enough to express how much I love you all. I hope you know. Cris, Eddie, Miguel, and everybody, I think you do know. Thank God for that, and for you.

Tina and Meera, this book is yours with all my love. And Amit: To say that your love has made so much possible doesn't even begin to cover it. Wow. And thank you.

Cecilia Muñoz spent two decades at the National Council of La Raza (now UnidosUS), followed by eight years in the Obama White House, becoming the country's longest-serving director of the Domestic Policy Council. She is now the vice president for public interest technology and local initiatives at New America, a think tank and civic platform in Washington, DC. She is the recipient of a MacArthur Genius Award for her work on civil rights and immigration. She lives with her husband in Maryland.